# VISION
## OF
# LIFE

# VISION
## OF
# LIFE

## BALANCE IN LIFE AND...

Edited by Dr. Tahirih Foroughi

THE
DONNING COMPANY
PUBLISHERS
20TH
ANNIVERSARY

The Donning Company/Publishers
184 Business Park Drive, Suite 106
Virginia Beach, Virginia  23462
        Steve Mull, General Manager
        Barbara A. Bolton, Project Director
        Tracey Emmons-Schneider, Project Research Coordinator
        Karen Kraft, Editor and Designer
        Elizabeth B. Bobbitt, Production Editor
        Tony Lillis, Director of Marketing

Library of Congress Cataloging in Publication Data:
Vision of life: balance in life and — / edited by Tahirih Foroughi.
        p.    cm.
        Includes bibliographical references.
        ISBN 0-89865-894-2 (soft cover : acid-free)
        1. Accounting—Literary collections.  2. American literature—
20th century.  I. Foroughi, Tahirih.
PS509.A25V57    1994
811'.5408092657—dc20                          94-29218
                                          CIP

*This book is dedicated
to the memory of
my late student,
Charles Olin Norton.*

# TABLE OF CONTENTS

# TABLE OF CONTENTS

# Preface

It has been said that "the place of any nation in history is determined by the quality and standard of the works its poets, philosophers, artists and scientists have contributed to the world..."[1] at large. It has also been said that the essence of all of the advice and guidance for a happy and successful life can be summarized in one word: **balance.** Balance creates satisfaction and content. Balance in all aspects (and the interaction thereof) of one's life, i.e., thoughts, deeds, and words, gives one perspective and a sense of proportion and harmony which guides one's life and makes one a better person in all one's activities. This book is about this balance—creating a balance through the marriage of the soft (poetry, arts, and other gentle areas of human knowledge and human effort) and the hard (accounting, sciences, and other similar technical fields.)

My interest in this topic can be attributed to my childhood and my family life. I am the firstborn in a family of six children, three girls and three boys. My mother was a poetess whose love of poetry helped her cope with many difficulties of life, including the untimely death (at the age of twenty-five) of her only brother. My father was a chemist by education, but at thirty years of age he changed his profession and became an accountant/banker.

I was raised in this family of odds, yet of balances. From childhood I was introduced by my parents to both poetry and accounting, or, in other words, two examples or symbols of the soft and the rough sides of life. In my teenage and youth years, I memorized poetry mostly for relaxation and entertainment purposes and sometimes played a game called *mosha-ereh*, or exchange of poetic verses, with my mother and/or my friends. As I mentioned above, I was also introduced to accounting by my father who would—from time to time—explain to me the practical side of accounting and give me assignments from real-world cases.

In college I studied business and accounting and then worked as a financial and project analyst for a World Bank-affiliated development bank in Iran. Meanwhile I married a high-school teacher, and we soon had three children (twin daughters and a son). Later, at the encouragement of my husband, I went back to college and continued my higher education in accounting and related areas, attending the University of Tehran, Stanford University, and the University of Oregon, from which I received a Ph.D. in accounting in 1975.

During the past two or three decades I have taught accounting in several major universities and their related programs in Iran and the United States. I have also published several books and many articles. The latest school at which I have taught is the American Graduate School of International Management (Thunderbird), which is a symbol of international cooperation and understanding, and to which I am dedicating "The Same Essence," which appears in this volume.

Although I had written a few poems in my childhood and teenage years, I had never seriously pursued poetry. However, in my thirties I started reading and writing poetry more seriously. This gave me the calm and serenity needed to excel in accounting and created for me a wonderful and pleasant window which helped me to temporarily escape from the hard rocks of the land of accounting, to take flight into the pleasant and gentle breezes of the sky of poetry, and to focus on the distant Point of Arrival where the harsh land (of accounting), the gentle sky (of poetry), and the ocean (of serenity) met, became one, and created a **balance.** This point of arrival/balance can be called "the point of Oneness"— meaning that in the universe all is one and represents Life's Essential Oneness.

Several years ago I started requiring or encouraging my accounting students to write or prepare some kind of creative work related to accounting. This work was worth a very minute part (only 1 or 2 percent of the student's total score) for grading, so I did not expect much student enthusiasm. However, I was pleasantly surprised to witness the creative interest which poured in. Some wrote creative papers and articles, some did artwork (drawings, pictures, cartoons, posters, etc.), some made music and wrote songs, some made games and puzzles, some wrote satire, scenarios, and plays, and some created and wrote poetry.

A small sample of these works is what has made this anthology and is printed herewith with the permission of the creators of these works. The marriage of the soft (gentle) and the rough (harsh) has been experimented with by many educators and professionals throughout the history of human endeavors. "If more politicians knew poetry," said President John F. Kennedy, "we would have a better world." Omar Khayyám, the famous, internationally known Persian poet of some thousand years ago, was also a mathematician, a philosopher, an astronomer, and an expert in many other fields of human knowledge. Books and articles written about Khayyám and his works total more than two thousand volumes in more than ten languages.[2]

Today a good number of professors in varying fields encourage their students to use their imagination and creativity. William Sharp is a professor of economics at Stanford University and the author of a theory that won him a share of the Nobel Prize in economics in 1990. One of his former students, Vlae Kershner, wrote about a class he took from Sharp:

> In the fall of 1981, I took a class from Sharp, the "poets" section of the required Stanford Business School course—gasp—microeconomic theory. That is the place they put jazz musicians, ex-sportswriters, and other humanities types who would never survive the calculus that economics courses typically require.[3]

After explaining several examples of how this course is taught, Kershner writes:

> In looking back nine years later, somehow I think that we "poets" got a more lasting economics lesson than the calculus freaks.[4]

Maxine Greene, professor of philosophy and education at Columbia University's Teachers College, specializes in the imagination, the arts, and in calling teachers, students, and anyone else she meets from mental and emotional slumber to "wide-awakenness."[5] Greene believes that the arts lift human beings from indifference and numbness to what is going on around them.[6]

Roger Doost, professor of accounting at Clemson University, is an avid lover of poetry and a poet himself. Three of his poems are included in this anthology.

Finally, the bringing together of poetry and accounting in this anthology gives us a chance to review and examine the similarities between these two major fields of human effort:

Poetry is an art of balances and rhythms.

Accounting is a field of balances and rhythms.

In poetry we have the stanza for balance and the verses for rhythm.

In accounting we have debits and credits (the two sides of the transaction) for balance and the period of time (the week, the month, the year) for rhythm.

Poetry is often considered to be a lonely art, as it is so intrinsic to one's soul. Accounting is probably a most lonely field, since the accountant experiences more paper and computer contact than s/he experiences human contact.

Through the bringing together of these two areas of human endeavor, we hope to bring to each one separately, and to the two together, a sense of unity and oneness which will extend beyond the mere temporary arena and will contribute to a better functioning of those involved in these areas.

As said by a poet who contributed to another anthology which I edited:

"Upon receipt of your letter and especially while reading through your introduction, table of contents and your own process of poetry I felt a tremendous sense of unity with the other poets listed...."

She further wrote:

"This is a special feeling because often poetry can be a lonely art...."[7]

# DEDICATION

One of the contributions to this anthology is a poem by Charles Olin Norton. Charles was an excellent student of mine in a Cost and Management Accounting class at Thunderbird. Charles left this world as the result of a traffic accident. His parents lost a wonderful son, I lost an excellent student, his friends lost a visionary, and Thunderbird lost an active, serious, and intelligent alumnus.

This book is dedicated to Charles. The memory of his dedication to balance, excellence, and dignity will always be with those who knew him. I am thankful to Charles' parents, Mr. Howard George Norton and Mrs. Ann Fisher Norton, who have contributed to this anthology through their ideas, words, thoughts, and friendship and by agreeing to the dedication of this anthology to the memory of their beloved son, and by writing the introduction as well as the eloquent conclusion which discusses Life and Death emphasizing that Life is like a piece of art which blooms into eternity once it is complete. They are true examples of balance in life. I feel honored to know them and to have been inspired by their serenity and dignity.

# ACKNOWLEDGMENTS

I also wish to offer my humble gratitude to the loving memory of my beloved parents, who not only introduced me to accounting and poetry but were also symbols of excellence from whom I learned about dealing with the ups and downs of life, a lesson which has become extremely useful throughout the days of my life.

I would like to thank my students whose contributions are reflected in this book as well as my students at large who have been my inspiration during the past thirty-plus years of teaching and writing.

I also thank my children, son-in-law, and grandchildren for being my inspiration, always. And I am grateful to my brother, Dr. Roger Doost, for contributing some of his poetry to this anthology.

Last, but not least, my gratitude goes to my husband, who—for the past thirty-seven years—has helped me keep my balance.

—*Tahirih Foroughi, Ph.D.*

# NOTES

1. Heshmat Moayyed and A. Margaret Arnet Madelung, in *A Nightingale's Lament, Translation of Selections from the Poems of Parvin Etesami (1907-41)*, Mazda Publishers, Lexington, KY, 1985, p. iii.
2. *Robaiate Hakim Omar Khayyám*, Kavian Publishers, collected by Teymour Borhan, Tehran, Iran, Introduction.
3. Vlae Kershner, "In Sharp's Class, even poets learned Microeconomics," *Stanford Business School Magazine*, December 1990, p. 4.
4. Ibid.
5. Maxine Greene, *Arizona Republic*, October 29, 1990, p. 1.
6. Ibid.
7. *My Calamity is My Providence*, compiled by Tahirih Foroughi, 1984, p. 6.

# INTRODUCTION

We would like to take this opportunity to thank Dr. Tahirih Foroughi, who is on the faculty of the American Graduate School of International Management and is the editor of this anthology, for her generous invitation that we write the Introduction as well as the Conclusion to this collection of literary pieces: a most gracious act of an exceedingly gracious lady.

In this Introduction and in the Conclusion we will explore the relationship among three topics, as they pertain to this anthology: Dr. Foroughi's vision of Life, the death of our son, and the nature of Art. This collection of literary pieces is the artistic creation of Dr. Foroughi's students. As we shall see, the reason for their individual creation and their collective publication is the fact that her philosophy of Life is reflected in both cases. The occasion for their composition is her requirement that her students give an artistic expression of their experience of her course in Cost and Management Accounting. The occasion for their publication is the sudden and untimely death of our son, Charles Olin Norton, who had been one of Dr. Foroughi's students and to whom the anthology is dedicated. The publication of this collection is a testimony to Dr. Foroughi and a memorial to our son as well as a tribute to her students.

We believe that this anthology is unique and has a much-needed message for our time. Dr. Foroughi's vision of and reverence for Life's essential oneness, as a life of unity and integrity, is the theme of this book. She believes that Life, both in its corporate form of society and in its individual form of the person, is by nature whole and that its wholeness is realized when it is complete. To be whole and complete is to possess the balance of the ontological and the existential, of Being and doing, such as the balance between the affective and the rational, value and fact, art and science, the concrete and the abstract, the heart and the head, the feminine and the masculine, spirit and matter— that is, the unity of Heaven and Earth. For a person or society to be otherwise is to acknowledge only part of reality and, thereby, only half of Truth. The brokenness of persons, society, and the world is healed by the balance of wholeness and completeness, for to heal is to make whole.

To a large extent, Charles' life was an expression of the balance and wholeness of Dr. Foroughi's vision and, therefore, an image of that vision. He had a quick, analytic mind and a warm, caring heart, which combined to form a rationally articulate as well as an aesthetically and morally sensitive man. Charles was able to penetrate to the depths and grasp the subtleties of meaning and truth, whether of ideas or events, and, having rationally comprehended or affectively apprehended them, he had the courage to act as their meaning or significance dictated.

As an undergraduate student at Drew University, Charles pursued a double major in economics and art history and graduated *cum laude* with an A.B. degree. During his college years and in line with his double major, he completed summer internships with Christie's Auction House, New York City; with the Corporate Art Collection, Forbes

Magazine, New York City; and with Merrill Lynch Futures, Inc., New York City. This dual interest was the focus of his junior year abroad, at which time he studied the economic and political integration of the European Community at the Institute d'Etudes Europeenes in Brussels and studied art in Paris with the Paris summer program of Southern Methodist University.

Following graduation and prior to beginning graduate work at Thunderbird, Charles was employed in the Office of the Comptroller of the Currency, Administrator of National Banks, in Washington, D.C., where he was on the staff of the Senior Deputy Comptroller.

During the eight short months that he was at Thunderbird, Charles rapidly became involved in campus life: as a teaching assistant in the Computer Center, as vice-president of the German Club, as an active participant in the Finance Club and the International Christian Fellowship, and by reinstating the T'Bird Cycling Club. As members of the faculty and student body repeatedly emphasized, he will be remembered for his energy, intelligence, generosity, wit, enthusiasm, sensitivity, sense of humor, and happy disposition. By granting him the degree of Master in International Management posthumously and by establishing the Charles Olin Norton Memorial Lectureship in Corporate and Business Ethics, Thunderbird has acknowledged both who Charles was, as a person, and his enthusiastic and unique response and contribution to the life of the school.

As is the case with many tragic events and seeming ill winds, there comes a redeeming event—and so comes this anthology. It is because Charles achieved to a remarkable degree unity and wholeness in his life, thus giving it integrity, that his death is the occasion for its publication and is the reason for its dedication in his memory. As has already been indicated, and in keeping with her vision of Life, Dr. Foroughi requires of each student in her course in Cost and Management Accounting some artistic expression relevant to the subject matter of the course. Some students choose the medium of language, in the form of poetry, essay, or short story, as their means of expression. By way of these artistic pieces, her students give a balanced response to their experience of her course, in which both the rational and the affective are acknowledged, create a balance, and are expressed.

—*Howard George Norton*
*Ann Fisher Norton*
*December 1993*
*Baltimore*

## The Accounting Collage

—*Thomas C. Bidwell*

# Vision of Life

*For my students*

Life is beautiful
It is a gift given to you at birth
It is a gift of love
given to you
at no cost

You need to take care of this gift
Cherish it
Nourish it
and:
> Have a vision for it.

Give it meaning
Give it strength
Give it tenderness
Give it life itself
Give it love

Help it grow
Help it become useful
Help it become a means of true human advancement
Help it to become a true part of you
Become one with it

Make it a tower of strength
Yet of gentleness

Make it a full life
But, full of goodness and kindness
and of effort
true, sincere effort.

Become a true member of the world of humanity
a well-wisher of all humankind

Become a symbol of truthfulness
of friendship
of service
of awareness

of honesty
of cleanliness
of purity
of perseverance
of aim and purpose
of clarity of mind
and of sincerity of action.

Show reverence for your life
It is the only life you have
Stay away from all bad
and stay as close as possible to the good and goodness.

Remember your life was given to you whole
so,

> keep it whole
> and maintain its wholeness
> so that
> when you leave this world
> young or old
> your life is not just over or finished
> your life is COMPLETE

Show true action and act truthfully
Show love and be loving
Show service and be of service
Show strength and be strong
Show honesty and be honest

Reflect care and be caring
Reflect happiness and be happy
Reflect contentment and be content
Reflect respect and be respectful
Reflect healing and be a healer

Make sure your life has a purpose
Make sure your life has a significance
Make sure your life has a meaning
Make sure your life is full of joy, for you and others
Make sure your life is a TRUE life

Thus you will embrace unity
Thus you will embrace dignity
Thus you will embrace esteem
Thus you will embrace completeness
Thus you will embrace wholeness

Make your life a full life
But, only full of goodness
and of effort
True, sincere effort.

Make your life a complete life
whether it is going to be short or long
It is not important how long you live
It is important:
> how you live
> why you live
> what is your purpose in life
> what mission you have for your life
> and what are your actions in life

Be a visionary
Have a vision for life
A vision of fulfillment
A vision of true life
A vision of Oneness

So you will leave this world complete
And you will always be remembered
As a complete work of art.
> —*Tahirih Foroughi*

# *Who Is A Poet?*

A poet,
Takes the face of life;
Holds the thread of love;
And the needle of hurt;
And weaves the sheet of desire.

A poet walks in the garden of life and molds emotions;
Hurt into joy;
Tears into pearls;
Death into life;
Cry into laughter;
Bondage into freedom.

Despair into hope;
Hope into promise;
Promise into belief;
Belief into conviction.

A poet fishes at the sea of life and finds;
Understanding from superstition;
Tolerance from prejudice;
Love from hate;
Civility from fighting;
Freedom from jail;
Flowers from thorn;
Singing from shouting;
Order from disorder.

A poet climbs the mountain of life and,
Observes rivers, lakes, and oceans with appreciation;
Smells flowers, gardens, and trees with exhilaration;
Hugs Europeans, Asians, Africans, and Americans with anticipation;
Talks to theists, atheists, and agnostics with inspiration;
Loves Blacks, Whites, Reds, and Yellows with expectation.

A poet weaves thoughts into poems;
Poems touch our hearts;
And our spirits are enriched.
  *—Roger K. Doost*

# *My Feelings About Accounting Changed*

The first time I was confronted with the mysteries of accountancy I was supervising a small rural development project for the Peace Corps in Zaire. Since the money for this project came from the U.S. government and since my name was on the project proposal as "Le Responsable" I felt it my duty to, well, look at the books before I took off at the end of my two-year stint.

These books were being kept by the Zairian "Responsable," who was my best friend and only neighbor and, I repeat, I was auditing his work.

He was also the only reasonably successful local merchant in the village. At night he usually sat by the kerosene lantern in his thatched-roof house and taught himself accounting from a very dated, blurry, mimeographed manual.

One night after dinner we undertook the audit. His wife brought in a second lantern. I wondered if already he suspected that I wouldn't shed much light on the meaning of his toil.

I leafed through the various notebooks with dignity and self-respect. My eyes were binoculars of shrewd perspicacity as I surveyed the figures. Only for a few seconds did my gaze glaze over and reveal the confusion in my brain.

In retrospect, I think that I was looking at the General Journal along with Ledger accounts for things like Improved Sweet Potato Seed Acquisitions and Inventory of Iron Hoe Heads. My friend patiently explained everything to me, and by the end of that evening I had some idea of what meant what. Then, since the nearest photocopier was about 400 kilometers to the south, he devoted a few nights recopying everything by hand so I could take it to Kinshasa to show it to the U.S. government folks who had provided the fund.

They were all very impressed by "our" bit of accounting. Their dignity and self-respect was mingled with the same dose of shrewd perspicacity that I had shown two weeks earlier to my friend. I alone noticed that I goofed a bit in explaining how a certain number of hoe heads in the Journal also showed up in the Hoe Head account. But at this, their eyes didn't even glaze confusedly; they were real pros.

That experience is what made me decide to study business.

In a letter I received last week, my father reminded me of how much my feelings toward accounting have changed. He wrote: "We do read about your doings with great interest and I must admit that the prospect of you serving as TA [teaching assistant] in accounting was no small surprise. I alway felt that the future is unpredictable." He would have been less surprised had I announced that I was pregnant.

I believe that it is important to apply accounting procedures to everyday situations, so:

**"Accounting and Me"**
—the concept—
Balance Sheet
November 30, 1989

*Assets*
Current

| | | |
|---|---|---:|
| Accounts Receivable | grade for computer project | 5 |
| Sleep Receivable | in hours | 30 |
| Raw Mat. Inventory | a book, a calculator | 70 |
| Finished Goods Inv. | creative statement | 2 |
| Total Current | | 107 |

Fixed

| | | |
|---|---|---:|
| Plant | six yellowish houseplants | 14 |
| Property | wife (oops) | 24 |
| Equipment | spatulas, pots, pans | 12 |
| Total Fixed | | 50 |

| | | |
|---|---|---:|
| Total Assets | | 157 |

*Liabilities*
Current

| | | |
|---|---|---:|
| Accounts Payable | third exam | 31 |
| Quality Time Payable | many hours to wife | 23 |
| Water Pourable | to all six houseplants | 26 |
| Total Current | | 80 |

Long Term

| | | |
|---|---|---:|
| Mortgage (Educational) | to Profs. Hoshor & Foroughi | 15 |
| Bond (quality paper) | to stationery store | 2 |
| Total Long Term | | 17 |

| | | |
|---|---|---:|
| Total Liabilities | | 97 |

*Owner's Equity*

| | | |
|---|---|---:|
| Preferred Stock | 20 head Jersey Milk cows | 20 |
| Common Stock | 100 head Nevada scrub-eaters | 30 |
| Retained Learnings | 20% of last exam | 10 |
| Total Owner's Equity | | 60 |
| Total Liabilities and Owner's Equity | | 157 |

7

Variance Analysis

Calculations for a few of the most pertinent variances follow:

1. Total Course Grade Variance (note—standard grade is "C" = 2.0)

(std. grade x no. of courses) - (act. grade x no. of courses)

$\quad\quad$ (2.0 x 4) - (3.5 x 4)

$\quad\quad$ 8 - 14 = -6 Favorable

2. Total Course Load Variance (also "Course Quantity Variance")

(std. quantity) - (actual quantity)

$\quad\quad$ 5 courses - 4 courses = 1 Unfavorable

3. Study Time Quantity Variance

[(std. quant.) x (act. chapters)] - [(act. quant.) x (act. chapters)]

$\quad\quad$ (3 hrs. x 19 chapters) - (2 hrs. x 19 chapters)

$\quad\quad$ 57 - 38 = 19 $\quad\quad$ Favorable from my wife's point of view

$\quad\quad\quad\quad\quad\quad\quad\quad\quad\quad$ Unfavorable according to conscience

4. Study Time Opportunity Cost Variance

$\quad\quad$ [(act. quant.) x (act. chapters)] x (st. opp. cost)

less: $\quad$ [act. quant.) x (act. chapters)] x (act. opp. cost)

$\quad\quad$ (2 hrs. x 19 chapters) x $5.00 $\quad\quad$ =$190.00

less: $\quad$ (2 hrs. x. 19 chapters) x $15.00 $\quad\quad$ =$570.00

$\quad$ = $\quad\quad\quad\quad\quad\quad\quad\quad\quad\quad\quad\quad$ $380.00

$\quad\quad\quad\quad\quad\quad\quad\quad\quad\quad\quad\quad$ Unfavorable

*Analysis of Results and Conclusions:*

It is of great interest that the grade variance has increased while course load variance has worsened. The two are likely correlated and if, as expected next semester, the course load increases, grades may suffer.

$\quad\quad$ There may also be some correlation between the Favorable reduction in hours of study variance and the Unfavorable increase in the Opportunity Cost Variance. The latter was due to getting married recently. Unfortunately, the Opportunity Cost can be expected to rise next semester with the addition of a fifth course, probably resulting in a worsening of the other three variances. All efforts should be undertaken to stem an increase in the Opportunity Cost—no further marriages under any circumstances.

$\quad\quad$ —Robert Lakos

# *Then I Woke Up*

It was a beautiful Friday morning.
Full of joy I opened my Accounting book.
The problems seemed easy and provided
$\quad\quad$ me with a sense of contentment.
Then I woke up.
$\quad\quad$ —Sven

# Ode to Accounting

Always begin with the company's mission.
Then you assume the proper position
to assure the accounting is done with precision.
The result you will have is a proper decision.

Why, you might ask, such concern for control?
The bottom line, profit, is what makes the firm whole.
Don't overlook but the tiniest mole
and reward will be great, also good for your soul.

Some say accountants count nothing but beans.
But crucial are they, to those with the means.
If your costs are bursting your company's seams,
check with accounting and realize your dreams.

Gross margin, net income, what contribution?
Can we achieve it without more pollution?
Discover your problems and learn the solution,
But follow the rules to avoid retribution!

Where is the variance? Who is performing?
We must be aware of impressions we're forming.
Keep costs in line or the boss will be storming;
do your darned best to make profits heartwarming.

The question is this: can we do more for less?
Which units are thriving and which are a mess?
Decisions, decisions, we don't want to guess.
Use your accountants and don't fail the test!

Creative accounting, it's easy to fudge;
juggle the numbers and give them a nudge.
But best for your conscience if thou dost not budge
from the tenets of CASB—it be the judge!

And so we are ending this journey through cost.
It's been quite a term; many paths have we crossed.
A word to the wise, if you hope to be boss:
Keep up with the reading, or you'll surely get lost!
  —Bill Baroody

## Allocated Costs

Allocated costs must be
A pain to each subsidiary.
Just when profits start to show,
They step in and seek to mow.
Segment incomes show the ability,
Of managers' responsibility.
Thus the common costs are set
Aside till segment goals are met.
Then they're added to the side,
To not affect each segment's pride.
The president must only view
The relevant in order to
Be just to each department's job,
Or he'll be hated by the mob.
Therefore, this all goes to show,
That allocated costs are not
Relevant to manager Joe,
Nor to the segment's profit plot.
            —*Ellen Antinucci*

## The Ghost of...

Sitting on my table at 12 o'clock at night
Glancing through my Cost Accounting book, gave me a big fright
With budgeting, process costing & factory overhead galore
I didn't realize it then, but I was only on chapter 4.

Only 20 more chapters to do, including chapter 10
Variances, transfer pricing, the stuff for the big men
Flexible budgeting seemed rigid to me
And the split ledger system, that's the last thing I wanted to see.

From the covers of Cherrington & Hubbard appeared a ghostly entity
Shouting direct material, direct labor, and return on equity
I asked the ghost what was in the final test
Break-even analysis, LIFO, and Just-In-Time management he said
But if you don't want to fail, young man, it's time you went to bed.
            —*Amit Badami*

## *The Battle Hymn of the Audit*

*(Sung to the tune of "Battle Hymn of the Republic")*
Mine eyes have seen the fury
    Of that awfully swift PC
It is churning out the awesome figures
    And printing for all to see
What will be the future
    Of this wonderful company
The audit marches on…

The boss is trembling in his corner
    Waiting for the auditors
To pronounce the final fateful word
    As he downs another Coors
Will he have a job tomorrow
    Or will his name be off the door?
The audit marches on…

Glory, glory, Arthur Andersen
Glory, glory, how thorough they've been
Glory, glory, Arthur Andersen
They've ripped this place to shreds!

The controller just had a breakdown
    And the coffee machine is out
Secretary's crying in the bathroom
    And refuses to come out
When suddenly down the corridor
    The pin-stripe suits march out…
The audit goes to lunch!

Now after several weeks have passed
    The staff is all but dead
And still the pin stripes punch their keys
    And slowly shake their heads
'Til finally one day it's over
And the auditor says, "Now, Fred,
The books all look OK!"

Glory, glory, Arthur Andersen
Glory, glory, how thorough they've been
Glory, glory, Arthur Andersen
They've ripped this place to shreds!
— *Beatrice Bernescut*

## *The Master Budget*

Oh, woe is me!
For I foresee
That I will forever be
Slaving over the master budget.

Midnight is near
There's no more beer
I'm all alone up here
Poring over the master budget.

As tomorrow looms
I fear my doom
In the executive boardroom
Fighting over the master budget.

Production's too low,
These fixed costs just won't go
There'll be hell to pay once I show
These figures on the master budget.

What! They'll scream
What can these mean
We'll just cut out the cream
To reduce the master budget.

But that's not enough!
We'll have to do all sorts of stuff
And the CEO will huff and puff
But we have to fix the master budget.

I thought the numbers were all wrong,
So I rewrote the figures all night long
But still the truth is that sales are weak, and costs are strong
As you can see in the master budget.

So what to do?
I put the question to you.
Surely there is someone who can solve the problem. But who?
The problem of our master budget.

We put out a call far and wide
To SUPER-ACCOUNTANT to come be our guide
With his help this company will be able to turn the tide
And resolve the master budget.

......and that's all, folks!......
  *—Beatrice Bernescut*

## LIFO, Hey, Out of My Life, Okay?

I'm awakened by my wife, oh, I've been dreaming,
She says, "Matt, what's this word LIFO you've been screaming?"
Tiredly she adds, "Go back to sleep, the night isn't yet lost,"
I look at her and say, "Let's talk Cost!"
She slaps me, but hard, and says "Matt, you're delirious,"
My reply is "In determining costs, Inspection Point is serious."
"Matt, with this silliness I'm starting to get fried!"
I retort, "The basil on tonight's fettuccini was Overapplied."
This hit home; "Enough! Close your eyes, now just lay back!"
"Lisa, how can I sleep knowing Chapter 23 discusses Payback!"
"But, Matt, Cost Accounting concludes with chapter twenty-two."
"No, no, it never ends: I'll carry Cost my whole life through."
Tears flow. "You said our marriage vows with less conviction…"
I regrouped. "Say, Cost surely can cause marital friction."
"No, there's more! Perhaps Cost is making the boys revert!"
"Could be; today they crayoned the letter 'T' all over my shirt."
"Inside each 'T' were the letters 'DR' and 'CR', did you notice?"
"Lisa, it's a miracle. Two-year-olds cannot possibly know this!"
"Dear, they even corrected your last test. Aren't they dears?"
This news was too much; I fell asleep in tears.
  *—Matthew E. Blyth*

# International Accounting (Accounting in Several Languages)

—Barry Chamberlain

14

## A Student Named Lynn

There once was a girl named Lynn Chappelear
whose feelings for Math were full of fear.
To avoid her fear she majored in English,
put numbers behind her and thought she was finished.

Lynn became a newspaper reporter,
in Washington D.C., a city of order.
She made her living with words and phrase,
and worked in D.C. for 6 years and some days.

But Lynn was interested in far away places,
international relations and foreign races.
There was a grad. school, out west, she had heard,
a graduate school called "Thunderbird."

She applied to Thunderbird but almost didn't come,
when she saw the quantitative courses, she had to run!
But several years later, Lynn got up her courage,
she quit her job to follow her urge.

Lynn became a student determined to win,
but then she met Prof. _____n.
She dropped his accounting course two different times,
then went to GCC and paid her fine.

After a year of baby Accounting at GCC,
Lynn was able to continue with her MIM degree.
It's her last semester and Lynn will graduate in May,
and if she passes Cost Accounting it will make her day!
      *—Lynn Chappelear*

## Numbers, Numbers

Numbers, numbers in my head
How many accounting books have I read
I couldn't believe what I said
"Change the balance sheets on my bed."

But, how much money will I make?
I've worked hard enough for goodness sake
My income statement might reflect
A promising profit, I suspect.

I better crunch my numbers more
Or all my money will go out the door
I'll reconcile my statement too
The financial period is brand new.
    —*Myung Ho Choi*

## My Thoughts on Accounting

**Accounting**—as defined by J. O. Cherrington, E. D. Hubbard, and D. H. Luthy, authors of *Cost Accounting: A Managerial Approach*—"is the process of recording, classifying, summarizing, and reporting the economic activities of an organization…to provide information to users [external and internal to the organization] of financial reports to assist them in their decision making."

At first glance, I would have to say that I do not find the themes of accounting and creativity to have much in common. The word *creativity* invokes images of artistry and the free flow of ideas, while the images conjured up by the word *accounting* are ones of dread and of numbers that paint only a financial (and therefore, incomplete) picture of some organization.

However, after studying accounting, perhaps one can concur that it is precisely these "numbers" that give impetus and shape to an organization's creativity. Creativity in our modern society (and an organization's creative goals and dreams) are nothing without these "numbers." Virtually everything in society has some "cost" associated with it.

The most interesting thing, perhaps, in the field of accounting, is that while there are standards and principles to follow, so much of accounting is based upon imagination (if you will) and estimation. Therein lies the creativity of accounting. Depending on how one estimates and presents the financial information of an organization, the users of such information will form varying impressions of the manner in which the organization is managed, and of its future direction.

After having studied something of accounting during my time here in Arizona, I still have to wonder why anyone would subject themselves to the seemingly mind-boggling and persnickety tasks associated with the accountant's job. However, I can certainly appreciate the need for the accountant's job, and the need for professionalism—combined with dedication to accuracy and fairness—in the field of accounting. Like the legal profession (somewhat, anyway), the accounting profession appears to be a "necessary" part of maintaining order in our society's organizations. Accounting is one of the foundations upon which an organization's objectives are grounded and realized.
—*Mark E. Czajkowski*

## *The Balance Sheet*

A balance sheet is tough they say,
But I can show you the easy way.
Just use the easy steps that follow,
And you will never have to wallow.
First check your wallet and count the cash,
Take careful note of all your stash.
Then carefully check who owes you money,
Even the balance from your honey!
Then take a count of the stuff you own,
Even the goods you got on loan.
This completes the upper part,
What now remains will ease your heart.
First sum up the balance that you owe,
Whether it be high or favorably low.
To this you'll add your equity,
And it will balance, you will see.
Now you know how to balance your sheet,
But if you have trouble, we can meet.
And for this short poem I do believe,
Two bonus points I will receive.
　　　　—*Richard Davis*

## C is for Costing

C is for **costing,** a process so dear
O is for **overhead** which shouldn't cause fear
S is for **sales mix,** we all had to calculate
T is for **transferred-in costs** which sometimes may irritate

A is for **actual costs** which are usually given
C is for **control** which should always be kept even
C is for **contribution margin** which cover fixed costs
O is for **output** with no units lost
U is for **unavoidable fixed costs** which cannot be reduced
N is for **normal capacity** or what should be produced
T is for the **total costs** of a particular activity
I is for **indirect costs** which lack traceability
N is for **non-routine,** *you* make classtime go fast
G is for **gracias,** or *thanks*—you've got class.
    —*Cecy DeReuil*

## Creative Statement

Accounting, accounting, what do I need to know?
Is it LIFO or FIFO, just how does the story go?
Do I make? Do I buy? Can't someone please help me?
The formulas are too difficult, and I never can agree.
Oh I budget my books, my accounts, and yes, my spending too,
But somehow I'm overdrawn this month again…oh well, nothing new!
The process is so simple. So easy. Piece of cake! So I'm told.
But they never took the tests, never suffered, and hey, I'm too old!
Too old to use formulas, too much to fill my head,
If my life ever depended on accounting, no questions asked…I'm dead!

Thank you, Dr. Foroughi, it's been a pleasure.
    —*Richard Wolf Furstenberg*

# Cross Accounting

**Across**

1. The level of sales volume at which total revenues equal total costs
4. Real expenses incurred
9. Operation (abbr.)
10. One of a product
12. 3.141592654…
13. A budget that is relevant to only one level of business activity
15. Small (abbr.)
16. Total overhead (abbr.)
17. (Std. Time-Act. Time) x Std. Rate (abbr.)
19. _____ forma statement
20. Future costs that are different under one decision alternative than under another decision alternative.
22. An alternative to beer at the Pub
23. Didn't tell the truth
24. Number (abbr.)
25. Fixed, _____ variable

28. "Fill _____ the blank"
29. "_____ your entries"
31. Total less expenses
33. Department that creates products
34. Calculation of yield on a bond, from current date until it is scheduled to be retired (abbr.)
35. A budget that contains a complete set of pro forma financial statements with detailed supporting schedules
37. Return on assets (abbr.)
39. The relative proportion of components in a mixture
40. Type of tree found near Flagstaff
42. The margin obtained from subtracting the cost of goods sold from sales revenue
45. An itemized estimate of the operating results of an enterprise for a future time period
46. …and so on, and so forth (abbr.)
47. An inventory cost flow assumption that the differentiates between costs of the previous period that are contained in a work-in-process beginning inventory, and the costs incurred during the current period (abbr.)
48. Gas, electric, water, etc. (abbr.)
49. Physical work
52. The cost associated with the next unit
55. A cost that is the inevitable consequence of a previous commitment
56. A rule established by Foroughi
57. The ongoing process of implementing management's plans and providing feedback of actual results so managers can make needed adjustments

**Down**
1. The recording of a nation's total payment to foreign countries, including its total receipts from abroad (abbr.)
2. As used in process costing, a measure of the work effort of a department, process, or operation. "_____ units"
3. A cost with immediate benefit that is recorded as an expense
5. A measurement, in monetary terms, of the amount of resources used to acquire goods or services
6. Amount used. "_____ amount" (abbr.)
7. Amount obtained as a result of adding
8. What we're studying
9. Job _____ cost system
11. How you feel after Foroughi's exams
14. What you want to balance on the balance sheets
15. A norm or normal amount of quantities or prices
18. "Put your name _____ the top of the sheet"

19. A writing instrument
20. A form of internal reporting that is based on the ability to control "_____ accounting"
21. A negative response
26. The sale price minus variable cost per unit
27. Analysis of written records of the financial status of an organization (abbr.)
28. A cost that is not directly traceable to the manufactured product
30. Costs that were incurred in a past period
32. European Monetary System ( __ __ S) (abbr.)
36. What finals do to the class
38. Not long _____ we started accounting
40. Classmate
43. In the near future
44. Amount
50. What's drunk most often at Thunderbird
51. An inventory cost flow assumption by which the cost of the last materials received is assumed to be the cost of the first materials issued (abbr.)
52. Management By Objective (abbr.)
53. A small rodent, or bad person
54. Where experiments are conducted (abbr.)
    —*Cheryl E. Aurand*

## *Alternative Thoughts on Cost Accounting*

As I approached her at the pub I wondered to myself, "What might be my **return on investment**?" Her **segment margin** looked interesting, but I still maintained a **margin of safety.** I hated the idea of not approaching and suffering potential **abnormal spoilage,** but I was fearful I wouldn't make a satisfactory **contribution report.** In addition, I wondered what her **activity base** had been? Well, I figured I could bear the **full cost** so I decided to expend the **direct labor,** be **flexible, budget** my time right, and perhaps I'd even achieve **cost recovery.** I used my never-fail **"high-low"** opening that went something like: "**high,** buy you a **low**enbrau?" She looked at me as if to say, "I've seen square before, pal, but you are about the **least of the squares** I've ever seen." At this point I figured I'd cut my **normal rate of loss** and get back into the **network flow,** but I didn't really have a **master plan.** Besides, my **level of aspiration** was in the **market basket.** I decided to try a **reciprocal method** and this time use my **fixed overhead;** after all, that is what it was there for. Besides, I didn't have any **defective units** nor was I a **gross margin;** all I wanted was a **breakeven point.** After regaining my courage I used my **discretionary costs** and made a **nonroutine decision.** This **segment** would require a lot of **out-of-pocket costs** that I couldn't afford. Anyway, we didn't share any **common fixed costs,** so I cut my losses, ordered another beer and went to look for an **equivalent unit.** After all, whose **lifo** is it anyway?
    —*Carl Gardner*

21

## Unaccountable Romance

She smiled, and I smiled back. I had an uncontrollable urge for variation.

After a quick breakeven analysis, I decided that her learning curves were the least square I'd seen, and I asked her how much lead time she needed to complete her sensitivity analysis of my independent variables.

She said I exceeded her currently attainable standards and was definitely no defective unit. We hopped into my new jalopy—one of those jobs with a split ledger shift system, double entry exhausts, and all aluminum overheads. Performance reporting on normal capacity of this rocket ship, for me, had made cost irrelevant.

We parked and checked each others' activity bases. She said I had a big margin of safety since she had adopted both the reciprocal and step methods.

But I felt this was definitely a nonroutine decision; a little voice told me this could be the matching concept I had been seeking. I asked her about becoming a joint product, but when she said her theoretical capacity exceeded most guys' flexible budget I got nervous. Then she asked if maybe I had an equivalent unit in the family so she could get an economic quantity out of this deal!

After a quick evaluation of my capabilities in the service department, her unavoidable fixed costs, and the possibility of me becoming just another expired cost in her mix variance, I opted to be the last in and first out of her life.

—*John Allan*

## The Accounting Puzzle

**Across**

1. Process of recording, classifying, summarizing, and reporting the economic activities of an organization
4. Revenue minus variable costs
6. Summary Account in the general ledger that is supported in detail by individual accounts in the subsidiary ledger

8. (Actual Index x St. Var. Overhead Rate) - Actual Var. Overhead
10. Costs that do not relate to any of the decision alternatives, are historical in nature, or are the same under all decision alternatives
12. Expression for indirect manufacturing costs
14. A spoilage that is caused by unusual or unexpected factors occurring in production
15. The costs associated with the next unit or project
16. Future costs that are different under one decision alternative than under another
18. The person responsible for all accounting activities within an organization
19. A type of budget which uses a formula to adjust budget cost at various levels of business activity
21. An account used to facilitate the accounting process which holds cost data until it can be transferred or distributed to other accounts
22. (Actual Price) - Budgeted Price x Actual Sales Volume
23. The financial executive responsible for all functions classified under money management
25. A criterion for management which refers to a norm or normal amount of quantities or prices to be paid for materials and labor required to make a product or provide a service

## Down

2. Outlay or expenditure of money to acquire goods and services that assist in performing business operations
3. Cost associated with a single unit of product
5. Itemized estimate of operating results
7. (Standard Direct Mat'ls for Act Prod - Act DM Used) x Std price
9. Sales - Cost of Goods Sold
11. Costs associated with a particular activity or limited to a specific category
13. A cost that can be traced to a single cost object
17. Costs that vary in total as the volume of production or sales changes
20. A form of interest used to calculate desired net income
24. A type of asset that is relatively more durable and can be used repeatedly in the production of goods and services
    —*Bernadette Cohen*

## Modern Times

A salesman for a computer company visits the accounting department of a large firm to which he had sold an extremely powerful computer a month before. When he enters the office he is surprised to see all the accountants working like madmen, rushing through the massive payroll, their only seconds of relaxation being the time they spend sharpening their pencils. In the meantime, the salesman notices that, stacked away in an open closet, the computer is still stored in its original box. The extremely sophisticated software he has developed for this company is displayed on a shelf overlooking the office. When he approaches the office manager he inquisitively asks:

—"Aren't you satisfied with your purchase?"

—"On the contrary, it is the best buy I have ever made!" answers the elated manager.

—"I don't understand," the puzzled salesman comments, "the computer is still in its box!"

—"I know, but since I have bought it, all of the accountants work much harder. Productivity has almost doubled! You see, I keep on threatening them that if they do not work harder, the computer will replace them all!"

—*Alan R. Hairabedian*

## The Accounting Recipe

**Ingredients Needed:** Paper, Accounting book with solutions manual, Time, Calculator, Professor, Sleep, More Time, Silence, Patience, a Quick Mind, Luck.

1. Prepare Quick Mind by eating a good breakfast after allowing to rest for 10 hours.
2. Select the best professor available (extremely important ingredient).
3. Mix liberally together: Accounting book with solutions manual, Paper, Pencils, Time.
4. Add the Quick Mind to above ingredients and let sit for Long Time in a Silent place. Do not allow loud noises to disturb the mix or whole thing will turn mushy and seek escape in the TV, Pub, Mall, etc.
5. Sprinkle continuously and liberally with plenty of Patience.
6. With luck you can have a "beautiful" piece of accounting with equal Debits and Credits.
7. Best Served *HOT*!!!!!!!!!!!!!!!!!!!!!!

—*Keith Hamby*

## Ode to Cost Accounting

Eons and eons ago lived a very cruel soul,
With a heart of stone and vision like a mole.
This sadist supreme
Fulfilled his ultimate dream,
And to the world he did bring,
That most horrible thing,
Which we all know as Accounting.
As punishment for my previous sin,
I was sentenced to a classroom where I couldn't win.

24

No literature could save me there,
I told all philosophy to beware.
Goodbye weekend fun,
Adios to slow days in the sun.
No more time for me,
Time to start praying for a B.

The first ordeal was to buy The Book,
It was said myopism would curse those who dared a look.
With a silver bullet and a garlic clove,
I held my breath and into the text I dove.
At first it was murky and cold,
I couldn't believe so many of these desk weights were sold.
Heavy, thick and black,
I wanted to take it back.
But I read on and on,
Slowly flipping the pages and beginning to yawn.
And then it appeared to me,
A sloppy script scrawled hard to see.
Believe it or not I read my name,
A personal note with a very big claim.
"For you, Mr. S. H., a chance to pass,
All you need is ear of wombat and lip of bass,
Or instead a promise to forever salute,
Every accountant, no matter how cute.
But first you need to recite,
The secret word and you better get it right."

Days passed and I screamed thousands of words,
"Open Sesame," "Hi-ho Silver away!", "Long live Thunderbirds!"
No time left for miracles, I thought,
And started again to read the book I bought.
Test just hours away,
Tomorrow most certainly was Doomsday.
Struggling with a T-account,
The frustration began to mount.
Finally at wit's end I tossed the book that was still new,
And screamed a most sacrilegious "FIFO you!"
Suddenly the room went dark,
Even old Rover started to bark.

Smoke filled the walls,
And a high-pitched voice asked "Who calls?"
Before me stood the most incredible geek,
With thick glasses resting on his beak.
Pencils in his pocket looked well-worn.
His floodwater pants were a bit torn.
"Well, whatdaya want?" he squealed,
After smelling his breath I reeled.
"Leave me, you nerd, you pest,
Can't you see tomorrow I got a test."
A smile filled his green face,
"A test which I could undoubtedly ace,"
He proudly boasted.
I knew it was true, but my goose was roasted.
"For a price I can give you the key,
The magic incantation which Foroughi told me.
Memorize it and your problems will disappear,
But you will have to bow to me for a whole year."
"No problem, you simp," I told him,
"Anything as long as I can still get my MIM."
The rest is history,
I paid the fee and earned my B.
Unsatisfied, you desire to know the Accounting password,
Well, don't ask me—go find that nerd!
　　—Steve Handelsman

## Accounting: A Creative Statement

If I had taken Dr. Foroughi's Cost and Managerial Accounting class five years ago, I would have had a much easier time in the work place. For five years, I worked in the area of project management and finance for R... International. Like most new college graduates, I showed up on my first day with a lot of enthusiasm, however, not much experience. I studied "Accounting 101 and 102," and had basically decided that accounting was for those people who had nothing better to do than spend ten hours working an accounting problem, and then 15 more hours recounting their steps in order to find the $3 error on their balance sheet. No, no, that was certainly not for me! I would never, never want to be one of THOSE people. I considered once, that perhaps accounting was a communist plot to drive us all to the point of insanity so that they could someday take over the world. Where is all of this leading, you ask? While in Dr. Foroughi's Cost and Managerial Accounting class, something happened. I realized that accounting was so much more than debits and credits, T-Accounts and endless unbalanced balance sheets.

26

From the first day of class, I saw useful tools that could have made my job at R... so much easier. I can look back on the endless hours I spent at R..., especially in my first year, trying to figure out things like flexible production budgets, applied overhead rates, standards, etc., so that I could make sense of the information in my analysis. If I had only had this class five years ago, I could have performed my job much more efficiently early on in my career, and at a much lower cost to the company. Last year I was assigned a project by senior management to perform an investment analysis on one of their production departments which had produced transformers for many years. My assigned task was to determine whether it was more profitable to make or buy the product, to determine the department's overall contribution to the business segment, and to advise management on whether the production facility should be shut down. If I had only known about the various make or buy methods, contribution analysis, etc., not only would I have saved a lot of time and money, but I could have put together an excellent presentation to assist senior management in their decision. As it turned out, I was able to do a good quality analysis and provide the company with some very good options, however, only after a lot of time and money. Never again will I underestimate the value of accounting and the useful information it can provide in the managerial process. I now see it as an essential part of the management process and I will leave Thunderbird knowing that I have the tools I need to make good managerial decisions in a timely and cost-effective manner.

—*Lori Henderson*

## *There Once Was a Class Called Cost*

There once was a class called Cost
In which I feared I'd be lost.

Direct Labor and Materials,
Factory Overhead too.
Fixed Costs, Variable Costs—
How to choose 'tween the two?
Profit Analysis and budgets
Were not too hard to bear,
But the journal entries on the second test
Had me pulling out my hair.

Variances and segment analysis
Were kind of fun to do:
I always learned much more
By doing my homework before you.
Cost Accounting has taught me very much
Though much I deduced:
Allocate the costs of manufacturing
To the number of units produced.
  —*Francois D. Henry*

## *My Troubles Are Mounting*

As if there weren't problems enough,
My troubles are mounting,
With projects for marketing and tests in accounting.

So if anyone asks me
What's life's biggest bummer,
I'll tell them it's being stuck
in Glendale all summer.

But when it came time
to figure the cost,
Without Prof. Foroughi
We would have been lost.
  —*John Hensley*

## T-Account Nightmare

—Tomoko Ando

# *The New Manufacturing Cost Accounting?*

Today, most manufacturing executives agree that the U.S. desperately needs a new manufacturing philosophy. They now acknowledge that simply trying to revamp the current system is not enough in this fiercely competitive field. They also realize that continued revamping will only put them further behind. So too could be the fate of the current manufacturing cost accounting system.

The present cost accounting system was developed on a seemingly solid and indestructible foundation. But over time, as is the case with many other well founded theories, some questions have been raised as to its legitimacy. When this system was conceived, direct labor was the largest single manufacturing cost behind direct materials. Consequently, the "cost of manufacturing" is equated to direct labor by cost accounting. Since the element of direct labor is becoming increasingly less influential, it would seem some other unit of measurement is needed. Current cost accounting theory only accounts for the "cost of production," and not that of "nonproduction." Therefore, this system can only evaluate cost savings on a per unit basis.

Given this limitation, it is unlikely that many product improvements and/or innovations, let alone process innovations, can be justified. Consider the following scenario. At a time when part consolidation is at the top of many engineering departments' lists, the marketing department has growing concerns with losing product differentiation and customer appeal. Therefore, some improvements/innovations cannot be justified under the present labor-based system.

Oftentimes, automation is a compromise between the above two objectives. It is easy to determine the benefits of automation as they relate to manufacturing economies of scale. But what about the less visible aspects. Such as, improved quality, reduced machine changeover time, and the near elimination of "nonproductive" time? These benefits figure into the product cost equation and should be evaluated on a unit per time basis. Herein lays the dilemma. As was mentioned, the traditional system measures the "cost of production" and not that of "nonproduction." Because of this, it is nearly impossible to apply these theories of labor-based accounting to time-related output. Therefore, labor appears to be the wrong unit of measurement for evolving automated manufacturing facilities. The new measurement of manufacturing cost accounting should therefore be time.

Nowadays, bad output often costs as much as good output, when considering direct labor and direct material. Therefore it would be safe to deduce that under these circumstances, the once traditional "variable" costs are now "fixed." If this assumption is made, then all costs are "fixed" and the only parameter both variable and controllable is the time it takes to manufacture the product. Therefore, anything that can reduce the process time should be termed a benefit and not strictly a cost.

Basing manufacturing cost accounting standards on time rather than on labor would force management to evaluate many factors not presently considered. Labor is a variable that can be increased or decreased as needed. But time is a constant, which if not utilized is lost forever. In this day and age, more so than ever, when time is lost, so too is money.

—*Douglas L. Henson*

## The Cost Accounting Rap

*For Dr. Foroughi: May your worksheets always balance.*

When your FIFO comes out over
and your LIFO comes out short
When your weighted average isn't
And you've lost your cost report
When your debits look like credits
But your credits ain't been used…

Then I think you got what I got—
It's those COST ACCOUNTING BLUES!
—*Richard A. Howell*

## Thoughts From a Creative Writing Major

The transition from Creative Writing to Accounting is not an easy one. There is no such thing as "Creative Accounting." People get arrested for that. Accounting, without a doubt, is rule-oriented, to be considered appealing by those who like explanations for everything, and to have everything in its place. It seems incredible to think that a simple double-entry concept first conceived of hundreds of years ago remains the foundation of our present-day system. Someone somewhere was rather persuasive. Someone was also not too bright. Writers at least get royalties.

Unfortunately, it seems the honor of "correctness" is magically bestowed upon accounts or statements which happen somehow to "balance" or to have numbers on the left side equal to numbers on the right (why that would seem so amazing I am unsure, since the numbers are recorded symmetrically throughout the process). Yet "balanced" has somehow been connected with correct such that correct is assumed to describe what is in balance. Says who? Personally, I prefer to have my exam calculations described as "in agreement or disagreement with the presumed answers according to the great accountant in the sky," rather than as "right" or "wrong." The world bats not an eye at the asymmetrical body of a giraffe, nor at the unique construction of a three-legged stool. Likewise, it is willing to tolerate both five- and six-pointed stars. Why then must Accounting always be two-sided and in balance to be thought of as correct?

Those who choose Accounting as a career might provide some clue to this obsession with balance and orderliness. On the whole, the breed does contain more than its share of introverts, as well as neat, methodical beings used to doing things according to a prescribed plan and without deviation. (Deviation might lead to unfavorable variance.) Yes, these are the same social misfits who perch on the end of the buffet table at a cocktail party and proceed to devour the entire bowl of potato chips, chip by chip, stopping religiously after scooping dip onto each chip to wipe the excess on the side of the bowl before chewing each victim chip 25 times. A real fun bunch these beancounters are. During daylight hours, Accounting provides the means for these tooth fairies of the business world to pursue their occupations with as little contact with humanity as possible, and with an equal amount of mystique (mystique, in this case, of the generic variety, as opposed to the famous Thunderbird Mystique). No one asks the tooth fairy why a giant molar should be worth the same dime or quarter that a small incisor is replaced with. So no one inquires why it is that A naturally must equal L plus OE.

Accountants then use this omnipotence to break accepted rules of behavior. Again, no one questions. Business people are cautioned not to use manila folders labelled "Miscellaneous," for example, for they quickly encompass the entire mass that used to be outside the filing system and therefore negate the need for any system at all. Accountants, however, boldly place things that they don't know what to do with in artificial accounts like "Income Summary." Sounds a lot fancier than "Misc." Furthermore, they have a knack for creating new accounts with undistinguishable names for the rest of what is unclaimed, or simply deem it "insignificant." ("I didn't write my paper last night, Professor X, as it seemed pretty 'insignificant' to me…")

Lastly, if we are to be fair, accountants do attempt to count things of significance, namely dollars. They use comforting words like "overhead" to describe those pesty costs that we never seem to be able to locate when we need them. And finally, their neat little reports and statements are generally legible and often even impressive, making us less uncomfortable about paying them some of those same dollars that they have gone to such pains to count. Now as for *economists*, with their spider web graphs and far-fetched theories…

—*Cheryl Johnson*

## Ode to Accounting on a Greco-Roman Abacus

Accounting can really hit you where it hurts,
it sometimes makes you feel dumber than dirt.
But if you work, and strive, and do your best,
you know in your heart that you'll pass Foroughi's test.
So you make the grade and look toward that graduation date,
and say "To get a wonderful job is my destiny, my fate."
So in accounting, that wonderful subject that we grew to hate,
Dr. Foroughi helped us all find something we could appreciate.
        —J. Todd Johnson

## The Cost Dragon

—Herman Guevara                33

## In the Back of My Mind

As I ride my bike I ask myself
What bothers me so that it affects my health?
I look around and am unable to find
It's Cost Accounting in the back of my mind.

So the final approaches in just two weeks
No wonder I can't sleep nor eat,
knowing that after the final is done
I'll go home for Christmas and have some fun.
    —David Kaliser

## Ode to Accounting

Roses are red,
This cost student is blue.
Materials, labors, overhead—
Who understands it, do you?

"Of course," says Teacher
"Who could be lost?
So easy is the concept
Of analyzing volume, profit and cost.

And don't forget variances,
Allocation and budgeting.
It's all such great fun—Why are the students fidgeting?"

"The answer is clear," say I
With a quizzical look.
"How can I do allocation and pricing
when I can't balance my checkbook?

I'm sure segment performance
and the like are important—
But if everyone understood it too well
Who would hire an accountant?

So, in sum (and no pun intended),
I must give my confession,
By not acing this class,
I'm supporting the accounting profession!"
        —*Alynne Landers*

## Cost Accounting Analysis

Initially, the return to graduate school, after nine years in sales and retail management, was fueled by the need to read a corporate report past the first page, and to effectively manage what was each year becoming increased responsibility in management. Of course, accounting is the fundamental skill we need to function responsibly with personal and financial decisions. It has been the greatest challenge I have faced academically, but accounting has also given me the tools I need to return to management and further my career.

Cost accounting directly relates to my goals of retail buying and eventually, owning or serving as president of a retail chain. My skills are excellent in human development, fashion merchandising and selection, sales force motivation, and communication, but without the ability to analyze costs and variables associated with overall retail efficiency, I would not feel confident or satisfied with my goals achieved.

This course directly relates to personnel and productivity measurement, stock-sales analysis, inventory management, profit/contribution margins and discounting procedures used in retail. Although I have not performed as well as I wish on examinations, I have learned more in this cost accounting class that I will use in my career than any other course. It has been an education to realize I am capable of understanding accounting on a daily basis, and that this concept will assist me in a successful career more than an "A+." The joy of a completed assignment and understood classroom discussion in cost accounting is an unexpected and much appreciated one.

Perhaps the most interesting and useful element of the course has been the analysis of variables and the methods used to determine the critical variable in an income statement. As a retail buyer, analysis is performed daily on each product line sales by region and store. The ability to establish overhead and factor costing methods in an effective and methodical fashion will be advantageous. I am truly grateful to have been a WB4140 student in your class and to have a working knowledge of these methods.
        —*Judy M. Lindell*

# Creative Statement on Accounting

This opportunity to do a creative statement about Accounting gives me a chance to express my feelings about a subject that I have feared from the day I first began an accounting course almost four years ago. I will relate how my perceptions of Accounting were first developed, give a history of my exposure to accounting, and finish by telling how I feel now about the subject.

In the spring of 1987 I took my first Accounting course at U. University. I had just gotten married and it was my first quarter at my new university. At the time I had no idea what I was getting into and all I knew about Accounting was that it involved numbers and a lot of meticulousness. My professor was actually just a graduate assistant who was preparing to take the CPA exam before leaving to California for his first job. He was a nice man but not very astute in the ability to communicate knowledge. Those in the course with previous knowledge in Accounting had a clear advantage over those of us who didn't, and I felt especially at a loss being a new student. Well, I made it through that first quarter and was ready to take the summer off. I was also involved in college football and was eager to enjoy a rest from school. Well, that rest from school came back to haunt me in the fall when it came time to take the next course in the Accounting series. I felt like I had forgotten everything from spring and yet we were moving on.

That second quarter of accounting proved to be a nightmare of T-accounts and three-hour tests. This time I was actually taught by a real professor but, unfortunately, his ability to teach fell in the same category as the first. Yet the major problem was my attitude about Accounting, and I knew that if I put the time into it I could understand the material.

The third and final quarter proved to be my favorite and the topic, Managerial Accounting, fell more directly into the realm of my major, Finance. The professor actually seemed to enjoy his job and could teach very well. Everything seemed to come together and even though I had some trouble with the final, I felt good about what I had learned. I could see my attitude changing about Accounting and I could even start to see its importance in business.

That was the end of my exposure to Accounting until I began this course this semester. I have to admit I was more apprehensive than not as I began the course as I remembered the bad experiences I had had previously. But as things would have it I have had the good fortune of taking this course from a professor who not only enjoys her job and can teach the subject very well, but also understands the fear that many students have when studying Accounting (like myself). For the first time I can actually understand how someone could actually work in an accounting profession and enjoy it at the same time.

My feelings about Accounting have gone through many changes, from fear, boredom, and little understanding to interest, greater understanding, and little fear. I am very appreciative to those professors who have the ability to show how such a subject can be enjoyed.

—*Russ Moody*

## Accounting

This poem is dedicated to the subject of Accounting, in its purest and simplest form; and to every branch, type, and offshoot derived from it.

...May I never have to see you again!

**A**  is for the acute pain caused to me all semester long. For the agony, anguish, annoyance, and animosity felt for this ancient system of ancestral, archaic numbers.

**C**  Could I conceivably clarify, construe, or communicate that Accounting is not common sense, but rather a form of commands, combined into a colossal combination of collective numbers that clog my claim to competency.

**O**  Outrageously oversimplified, yet overpowering and overrated. Overall, I would orate that the obnoxiousness outweighs the ostensible order. I feel like an orphan. Accounting is obscene.

**U**  The underlying competence has been usurped from my useful upperclass and once untroubled mind. This unpardonable, usurious subject has uprooted my unprotective and unschooled instincts, while unraveling my urban upbringing, with its unsavory usage.

**N**  Not allowed to negotiate, I was negligently knocked into this needless national narrative of numbers. I have navigated net income, net proceeds and net operating loss. I am now a number one nerd.

**T**  As tests transpired, I was teased by the trauma of once again, another transaction to transfer in or out. There must be a tradeoff for the torture tendered to my true and trustworthy teenage tolerance. Accounting is taboo, and I trust will taint even the tartest of tax evaders.

**G**  Thank goodness this game of garbage is not a test of my genetics or geniusness, but a gift from God to the guilty in order to germinate the ghetto.
Generally, I am genuine when saying—I would greatly gratify a good grade.
—*Stephanie Moss*

## The Story About a Count Ing and His Credits with the Little T-Account

Once upon a time in a faraway manual journal ledger, there lived an old and grumpy entry called a Count Ing. His home was located in the dark forest of Subsidary Ledger, and it was hard to find unless you knew your way. This was a really scary place with ghosts, goblins, and lots of Current and Long-Term Liabilities howling in between the trees. If you were daring enough to visit the count, you had better be prepared to use Job-Order costing as well as Process Costing in order to have a smooth cost flow through the forest. Most people were too scared to get into the world of Count Ing, they were afraid to get lost in all the cost determination, they fared the faith of a common cost. The Count was very lonely in his big old ledger. After the computers entered the world, his life in a manual ledger was slow and eventless. The Count would spend lots of hours calculating Direct Materials and Direct Labor cost, looking towards the faraway lights of the computerized ledger; he could see the dividends on the horizon.

In the Computerized ledgers of LOTUS, there were constant entries going on. T-accounts were coming and going like the ants in an anthill. Everything was so clean and effective; not a single variance had gotten away uninvestigated for the last accounting period. The balances were always as expected and if not they were questioned by the control accounts. Transfers from one account to the other were happening with the speed of a 286/12-10Mhz chip. In this hyper-effective accounting system, there was a little T-account called work-in-process for product type-X. She was a very unhappy little account. She felt she never got the chance to know any of her entries. They came in one evening and the next morning they moved on to finished-goods.

The little T-account felt lonely. She wanted to live her life in the old-fashioned, slow and comfortable life of a manual ledger. So she developed a plan. She was going to escape during the next audit, undetected in the enormous system of backups and floppy disks. And so she did! On January 31, she took off and headed for the closest manual ledger she knew: Overhead. She didn't really know if she would fit in or if she would get any entries, but she was in every way an unconventional little T-account.

The little T-account ran into the dark forest called Subsidiary Ledger. "No one will find me here," she thought. "I will be able to breathe in here," she thought. Just as she finished her thought, a Long-Term liability howled past her with a cold interest-rate. The little account screamed in fear. "Is this the life in a manual ledger? What have I done?!"

But someone had heard her call for help. Count Ing jumped to his feet, grabbed his anti-interest weapon, the money supply, and ran to the T-account's rescue. The brave, no longer so grumpy, Count Ing had soon paid off the Long-Term liability and curbed the interest rate. The little T-account was safe.

As they walked towards the lights of the Count's house, the old forest suddenly didn't feel that dark and cold any more. As the little T-account rested her head on the Count's shoulder, she knew that everything would be all right. The Count told her about all the interesting entries he had in his house: "Things happen rather slow here in the world of the manual ledger, you know, but they are much more human." Then the little T-account knew that she was in the right place. Here she would be able to live a good life in a normal speed. She knew that she would be able to contribute to the Costing System of some little company that couldn't afford to deal with the expensive demands of LOTUS. "The world is changing," she thought, "but we will always be important. A machine can only do so much; the manual method will always be needed in order to safeguard the accounting system."

The moral of the story: Computers and other technology are great means to make our lives easier, but let us not forget the basics. To know where you come from is key; without a knowledge of your past you have no future. This was my little thought about accounting.
—*Fredrik Motfeldt*

## A Business School in the West

There once was a business school in the West
Where students always tried their best
There were many courses that were blue chip
From Spanish, computers, and entrepreneurship
But the favorite class that was a bash
Was Dr. Foroughi's Accounting class
The students loved doing the homework
Variable and fixed costs they could not shirk
Contribution margins were the best
Except when it came time for the test
Cost of production schedules were not fun
At that point students wished the course was done.

But we know that accounting is useful
Especially when it comes to keeping the bank account full.
Now we're almost ready for management
But first we need to make one more adjustment
And get ready for hopefully the final test.
Keep up the good work, you're the best!
—*Matt Myers*

# A Diversion from Cost Accounting

On every Tuesday and Thursday of this semester
courage and stamina I would be forced to sequester,
For in the infamous room of the 31,
I attended a class which was a long way from fun.

This class I speak of—in case you are doubting—
was none other than that of Cost Accounting.
In this course of formulas, figures, and numbers,
I often forced my self from the deepest of slumbers.

And when at 10:10 the bell did toll,
I jumped from my seat and began to stroll
out of that class with its heavy textbook
towards the Spring morn and its blessed outlook.

"I am free for now," I'm thinking bemused to myself,
but only a moment do I wallow in my mental health
for despite my carefree glib and current laughter,
I must soon face my text and confront yet one more chapter!

These exams of Foroughi aren't easy for me—
especially her most recent—I refer to Test Three.
And despite my studies from dusk until dawn,
this was a test which required a time twice as long.

But aside from the hardships, the pain and the suffer,
this could have been a course infinitely tougher—
and I appreciate the professor's delightful, relaxed charm
for she eliminated much of the stress and its subsequent harm.

Yet enough of this nonsense and back to WB4140,
for the final fast approaches and is likely to be gory.
Only a few days remain to which I may study,
and the final three chapters still are, in my mind, quite muddy.
  —Tom Nootbaar

## A for the Grade

**A**    for the grade we've **all** worked for
**C**    because it's our favorite **class** this summer
**C**    for the **countless** hours we've studied
**O**    for the **overhead** allocation methods we've learned
**U**    since we finally **understand** the FIFO method
**N**    for the **normal** losses we've avoided
**T**    because we have the best **teacher**
**I**    for the **inventory** of knowledge we've accumulated
**N**    because we've reached our **normal** capacity for learning
**G**    because we're **going** to miss this class.
        *—John O'Connell*

## Accounting Through the Eyes of a Psychology Major

As a psychology major, I entered into the world of accounting with a rather closed mind. Stereotypically, accounting starts with a conglomeration of numbers and formulae which one has to somehow put in a coherent order. Pretty dull…huh?! Fortunately, I discovered that accounting only begins as numbers on various statements. The entire accounting process is much more involved. It deals with logic, interpretation, and, yes, even psychology.

For starters, one must be careful as to who actually is held responsible for the bottomline numbers (Responsibility accounting). This responsibility may be shared among individuals or be held solely by one employee. Regardless, one should not be held accountable for profits or losses that are not under his/her control or influence. Bad morale will surely develop if a worker is reprimanded under these circumstances.

Furthermore, accounting offers several methods for finding answers and interpretation. For example, the Absorption method versus the Variable costing method yield different net incomes. One needs to ask oneself, "Which is more applicable to the company?" and "Which result should be given to top management?" One also may have to make judgment calls, i.e., interpreting ROI (Return on InVestments) versus RI (Residual Income) results—is one clearly better, or is a combination of the two the best approach?

One also needs to set reasonable, attainable accounting goals in order to motivate the workers without intimidating them. Accounting methods need to be consistent, so the employee feels confident and knows where he/she stands, and where he/she needs to go. It is pointless to have an unclear goal and to let the employees work aimlessly.

For me, all of these **attributes of accounting** can also be **applied to life** in general. One must know his/her responsibilities and set clear, distinct goals, but also weigh any outside relevant factors that affect one's life and the degree to which they are important. (The key word is "relevant.")

This past semester was actually a pleasant surprise for me, because accounting now is not what I had initially made it out to be. It goes a great step beyond Balance Sheets and Income Statements.

—*Kelly O'Connor*

## Special Lyrics

Costs are by which a company will operate
And if they are kept low, top management will cooperate
Assuming revenues will fly
And capacity kept high
Things will go smoothly and your job won't keep you too late.

_____

Return on investment seems to be a popular measure
For managers, it's the difference between pain and pleasure
Although the calculations may be cumbersome
And the headaches quite numbersome
Reaching the desired rate puts a smile on the face of your treasurer.

_____

I once met an accountant while crossing the same road
We both burdened heavily while carrying our loads
My cargo was of lead
While his was in his head
Stumbling over balance sheets and ledgers as he strode.
—*William M. Olds*

## Definitions

**Ac • count • ing** n. 1. The system of recording and summarizing business and financial transactions in books and analyzing, verifying, and reporting the results; also the underlying body of principles and procedures. 2. The collection of financial data about an organization and the analysis, measurement, recording, and reporting of that information to decision-makers.

These definitions certainly do not sound incredibly inspirational to the average student. According to all of my friends while they were taking accounting in college, accounting made no real sense to them and they were never going to use it anyway. However, with all of their warnings in mind, I bravely entered into my first accounting class at Thunderbird with somewhat less than an open mind. I have been pleasantly surprised to find that it is not as bad as everyone said. The rules of accounting do seem random and inexplicable at times; however, accounting does make sense in a sort of confusing way. Although it is not the most fascinating subject, I still get excited when I get my debits and credits to balance!

Having an understanding of accounting is a very important, if not essential, part of any education. I find that my accounting knowledge is called into use in virtually every class that I have taken. The concepts that I have learned are essential to make rational economic decisions. Despite my initial reluctance to take accounting, I can honestly say that I am glad that I have done so and I know that I will put my newly found knowledge to use again and again.
—*Tracy L. Owen*

## *Not So Bad*

Actually, it's not so bad…
Chapter eight was the worst…
Can you believe it's almost over?
Only one more week to go…
Unusually fun for an Accounting class…
Nevertheless, I dreaded the homework…
Tell me when it's over…
If I'm still alive, we'll go to the PUB!
Not if I have to take the final!
God—Thanks for helping me through the semester!
—*Kathleen (Casey) Ramsey*

## Credit Love

The first time she walked through the huge glass doors of the building and into the pink marble lobby, Kim couldn't believe her eyes. She wondered why any company with posh offices in such a luxurious building would possibly want to hire her. Walking through those glass doors on her first day of work, Kim decided to quit doubting her value as an employee and enjoy her new surroundings. And besides, she was too excited about her new accounting job to think about anything else. The CPA exam had been a tough one, but she'd made it.

The elevators were crammed with people, perhaps ten to fifteen in each, so Kim chose to wait for the next one. She suddenly felt enveloped by a sea of dark suits. It was a scary feeling, like too many liabilities on a balance sheet. Kim looked around her and suddenly lost her breath. "I'll find the stairs," she thought, as her eyes anxiously searched for the stairwell.

Then her eyes met his, and she felt a soothing calmness chase away the anxiety. The sea of dark figures disappeared as they loaded themselves into the elevators and the doors closed. But Kim realized there was no time to wait for the next one, so she scurried toward the sign that said "Stairs."

The stranger ran after her only to find the door close in his face. She sprinted up the flights of stairs to her new place of work. Thoughts of spreadsheets filled with budgets, assets and liabilities, and tax laws filled her head as she walked through the reception area of the accounting firm. Having just received her CPA, she felt fortunate to have been hired by Arthur Young, a "Big Eight" accounting firm.

It was February, and soon she would be faced with the big tax rush. "What a zoo this place will be before April 15th," she thought. Kim was shown around the office, then led into her very own tiny office with half a window, the other half belonging to her next-door neighbor.

Kim had just started reviewing the financial statements of the clients she had been assigned when she heard a pleasant masculine voice say, "Good morning, mountain climber." She looked up to find the guy from the lobby. "I couldn't run up the stairs as fast as you did. I have a depreciation expense account on my legs now," he said and introduced himself as James.

They talked about falling in love with ledgers while working as bookkeepers in college, and about how fascinating they had found the whole idea of debits and credits to be. And they were pleased to learn they shared the same window.

The months that followed were filled with spreadsheets done using LOTUS 1-2-3, tax planning and reporting, tax credits, and FASB discussions. By April 15th, Kim and James worked closely together on the same accounts, both analyzing cash flows late into the night. They couldn't share enough financial statements just for the sake of being together.

One evening, over a working dinner in the conference room, James looked into Kim's eyes and said, "Will you marry me and balance the balance sheet of my life?" Of course, Kim accepted.

Whoever said accountants aren't romantic?

*Kim now works for Price Waterhouse.

**James is a managing partner at Peat Marwick.

—*Aramy Rodriguez*

## A Fine Aspiration

Accounting is a fine aspiration
> If you are into perspiration
The problems are hard, the solutions paltry
> You look like a fool if your answers are faulty
The chapters whiz by day by day
> It's easy to understand why your brain starts to fray
Budget variances and factory overhead are nice
> But I'd rather be dealing with a cold one on ice
So continue to figure your overhead due
> I'll be in the pub drinking a beer from Peru
Send me to Germany, Japan, or Tibet
> But don't ask me to interpret that damn cost of debt
This creative statement has gone much too far
> I've one last request before I get into my car
While I have no desire to become a CPA
> I'd sure make my folks happy if you gave me an A.
> —*Scott Ryley*

## I Took Cost Accounting

I took Cost Accounting and what did I find,
debits and credits cluttering my mind.
Income statements, balance sheets, expenses and revenues,
one has to account for all of them or sing the blues.

The exercises and problems helped for the exam,
but if not for the 9x5 sheet, I'd have been in a jam.
If it's one thing I've learnt from all this information,
it's the wealth that can be obtained from the correct application.

So I thank you, Professor Foroughi, for the knowledge you shared,
and the time you gave all of us showed that you cared.
Your teaching influenced my attitude toward accounting,
and will help in my future, whatever that might bring.
    —*Edward J. Shea*


## What Does Accounting Mean to Me?

What does accounting mean to me? Ben Franklin once said only two things in life are definite: death and taxes. He forgot to mention accounting. Accounting is necessary to calculate taxes, and for doing the final tally of one's estate.

Accounting is the last week of school.

It's playing the last inning of baseball when you know you've lost.

It's going through the graduation ceremony because your mother is there.

It's getting up early on Saturday morning.

It's reading the last few pages when you're tired.

It's shaving twice a day.

It's packing the car at the end of a vacation.

It's snow in April, or Phoenix in July.

It's running wind sprints in spring training.

It's learning to drive.

It's fuzzy radio reception.

It's reading classified ads.

It's adding up the master budget by hand.

It's attending class when there's a party on the Quad.

It's queuing to use the computer.

It's driving all day, or flying all night.

It's a flat tire.

It's bad news.

Accounting is something to be endured, perhaps appreciated, but rarely desired. You, however, are a very nice woman.
    —*Richard Singer*

## A Very Creative Statement

Throughout my lengthy academic endeavors
Mathematics has always been my weak spot
For in the manipulation & crunching of numbers
I've never really been too hot

Being a literal quantitative dope
This subject has always caused me great dismay
So at Thunderbird I had clung to the faint hope
That I could simply "waive it away........."

I was hell-bent on ducking this requirement!!
And thus at registration day in the TAC last summer
I approached the accounting department desk with fervent,
Being faced with taking accounting was a real bummer
(Besides, I wanted to take something a little more "funner"......)

"I'm marketing," I pleaded, "I really don't need all
        this," I said with a smile…
Professor _____n looked at me blankly, then rolled
        his eyes for a while

"Ok, alright," I begged, "but I did do 3100 & 3110."
Not impressed, he flashed me a look that said
        "Try again…"

And thus I embarked upon my journey into the wonderful
        world of accounting,
(Albeit I did so reluctantly: crying, screaming, and
        pouting…)

I must reinforce that I am a good student
I have three degrees and in several languages
        am quite fluent,
No, mine was not a problem of being lazy or dumb
Or that I preferred to daydream, sit in the sun and
        haunt the Pub.

Rather, my disinclination of accounting was due to the
      fact that I was simply "afraid"
For as I said before, numbers and my brain are not a
      match in heaven made……

But I studied hard and every class I attended
Hoping that my low aptitude in accounting soon would
      be mended
However, at the first exam, I about broke out in hives,
And my score reflected my turmoil: 25.5!!!!!!!!!!!!!!!

I sank into a deep depression and developed an aversion
      towards lead,
I recalled all of my hard work…then my grade point (!)
      and thought "Gasp! I'm dead!"
I didn't know what to do as I felt I couldn't do
      any better
"Don't worry," said Professor Foroughi. "You have time
      to raise it a whole letter!"

And then the strangest thing occurred;
My fear turned to rage
Thus I attacked my books and notes and memorized
      every page
I badgered poor Fredrick, and worked every problem
I hammered away till I was sure I could solve them
Then came the day that determined my fate:
The result was much better, well great, a 28!!!!

Confident & secure, I was determined not to earn less
& to finish exam 3 without a lucky guess
I couldn't believe it, it was too good to be true
and I began to break dance when I saw that 32!!!!!!
(And that's why I'm no longer singing the blues!)

And that, ladies & gentlemen, is how my cost accounting
    journey ended
And to believe that I survived it without becoming
    twisted and bended
Yet there remains one topic that I still haven't
    mastered
A certain statement that still leaves me quite
    flabbergasted
Although Professor Foroughi insists that all
    accountants are lazy
Take it from me, I disagree, they're really all
    just crazy................................
    —*Stacey Marie Snyder*

## *My Experience in Accounting*

In this paper I will try to explain my feelings towards accounting, cost accounting class in particular.

My first experience with accounting at Thunderbird started the first day I arrived here in Arizona. It was a hot summer day, and I was a couple of days late coming to orientation week because of my graduation from the undergraduate institution. Upon arriving at Thunderbird, I was given a list of classes that were waived and another list of classes that I needed to take in order to graduate. Looking at the second list, I figured out the classes that I planned to take, and most of them looked very interesting. I was very excited to start my graduate studies, but there was one big problem.

The problem was accounting. I had to take an accounting class in order to graduate from Thunderbird—"The most famous international business school in the world." The future looked very bright. I would have a good education, I would learn a lot, I would have a good job upon my graduation. Who could have possibly asked for anything more? But I would only realize a good future if I passed the accounting class of my choice. Now I had a real big problem. There was a big obstacle between my dreams and me: *Accounting*. I had decided to take an accounting course during my later semesters instead of my first semester. In doing so, I would also forget about accounting for some time and concentrate on my major area of studies.

The reality hit me when I looked at my progress sheet and saw that I was missing an accounting class to graduate. I could not escape from the reality any more and I had to choose an accounting course to graduate. Cost accounting sounded interesting, and it was supposed to be the easier one too. I signed up for the course and started taking it.

After taking the course I realized that my feelings towards accounting were based on my experiences with my financial accounting class that I took during my undergraduate studies. I found cost/managerial accounting class more interesting than the financial accounting. The cost accounting class was still a challenge for me, and I had to work to get a "B" average. However, I should mention that I enjoyed the class and learned a lot. The most important of all, I found out that the accounting class was not that much of an obstacle and it was bearable, even rewarding.

I will not be able to close my thoughts before mentioning the role of the teacher in making any class an enjoyable experience or a pain. In my case the first alternative was true. The positive attitude of our teacher, friendliness, understanding towards students really created a very enjoyable atmosphere for learning. Thank you for all efforts.

—*Unal Ozalp Sofuoglu*


## Another Ode to Cost Accounting

Dr. Foroughi is her name
And cost accounting is the game
We were told by the prof mentioned above
That cost accounting we could learn to love
And here we are approaching the end of the term
And with finals near we're starting to squirm
We're going for an extra point or two
So that's why we've made this song for you


Chapter by chapter we'll highlight the phrases
That make up our cost accounting bases
*Chapter 1*: Gives us an intro.
       And tells us exactly what we're gettin' into
*Chapter 2*: Now it's time to classify the costs
       We think that's where we began to get lost
          —Marginal
          —Sunk
          —Manufacturing
       Tell me, what does this all mean?
*Chapter 3*: Variable and fixed make up total cost
       And if you don't cover them you'll end up with a loss
*Chapter 4*: Income statements go from traditional to contribution
       Which only adds to our confusion
*Chapter 5*: The master budget was a real treat
       We couldn't even fit it on our cheat sheet
*Chapter 6*: We're told when reporting to show responsibility
       So throughout our budgets we demonstrate our capability

*Chapter 7:* We're told you have to at least break even
       If not you might as well start packin' and leavin;
*Chapter 8:* Job order costing vs. process
       Now we'll give you a brief synopsis
       Made to order or mass production
       You choose the one that will best function
*Chapters 9 & 10:* FIFO or LIFO, that's the dilemma
       Weighted-average adds to this problema
       Abnormal or normal are the types of loss
       The question is how to report it to your boss
       As those chips rolled past on the production line
       They turned into faces of past relatives of mine
*Chapters 13 & 14:* When allocating service department costs
       Reciprocal, direct or step are a must
*Chapters 15 & 16:* And now the moment you've been waiting for
       Although quite frankly Variances are a bore


And now that we've told our accounting story, my friend,
Please let us know when all of this will end......
    —*Jill Spott and Bettina Montalette*


## Accounting Is Like Religion

After much thought, I have concluded that accounting is like religion. It demands perfection in an imperfect world. That is to say, that as the various accounts must balance, so must we live our lives in balance. However, like most religions, accounting is also forgiving because it allows us to "round-off" our numbers in order to bring our accounts into harmony.

Like accounting, life has variances. However, in a spiritual sense our "variances" from morally acceptable (and thus, expected) behavior are recorded by the Great Bookkeeper in the Sky. In the end all variances must be justified or explained if the company is to avoid closure. Thus, as a firm with too many unfavorable variances can eventually go bankrupt, so can an individual with too many unfavorable spiritual variances go morally bankrupt.

As with most religions, accounting has a set of rules to guide the "would-be" accountant in his eternal struggle for perfectly balanced books. Accountants have calculators, textbooks, GAAP, and other accountants to help them with their work. In the same way we have the Holy Scriptures, friends, clergy, and family to help us. It is probably safe to say, that in either case, it would be impossible to be successful without such assistance.

At the end of the day, when the accountant's work is done, he closes his journal, shuts off his light, and leaves his work for another day. Within a few moments the thoughts about the difference that couldn't be reconciled or the flexible budget that wasn't so flexible are soon lost in anticipation of a quiet evening at home. However, unknown to the accountant, journal entries are still being posted to a ledger he carries in his soul. On the final day his Creator will audit his books and determine if the accountant has provided Him with a satisfactory return on his investment. If he has, he will be rewarded, but if he hasn't, he will be given a punishment greater than the most intense IRS audit.
—*James G. Taylor*

## *I Love Cost Accounting*

What is this process we use to manage our cost?
Since I am composing this poem it is obvious I am lost.

A true international manager must know how to settle an account.
They say the Cost Accounting system will provide the proper amount.

With all the costing and control for factory overhead,
I will never quit my quest for knowledge, not until I am dead.

Direct materials, variance analysis, and responsibility of reporting,
my desire to see it all clearly has become somewhat distorting.

The job order costing for a service organization or manufacturing firm,
it is not hard to understand, but it has caused me to squirm.

Let us not forget process costing with the weighted average or FIFO.
It all seems so easy, so why was my last test a big NO-GO?

The master budget, work in process, and break even point,
I doubt, very seriously, convicts study these endeavors in the joint.

The practical applications to Accounting are endless, without doubt.
It certainly will give my resume a little more clout.

Without these little debits and credits modern business could not survive.
When it all becomes crystal clear, I will certainly thrive.

So for the next four weeks, I will work even harder, and as always,
    attend every class.
I must understand the backbone of business, but more importantly,
    I must pass.
    —*Larry Scott Taylor*

## What I Think About Accounting

SIGNIFIC**A**NT
LOGI**C**AL
PRA**C**TICAL
**C**ONSERVATIVE
USEF**U**L
ESSE**N**TIAL
CATALYS**T**IC
CR**I**TICAL
INSTRUME**N**TAL
ENLI**G**HTENING
—*Chuan C. Teo*

## My Undergraduate Degree Was in History

My undergraduate degree was in history; I had never taken a business course before I came to AGSIM. Two classes that I particularly dreaded were accounting and statistics. Fortunately, neither subject has been as fearsome as I had imagined.

One thing that has both troubled and interested me about accounting is that managers can present information about their companies in many different ways while still conforming to generally accepted accounting principles. Before coming to business school, I imagined that, in accounting, there was one and only one correct way to present business data.

I have now learned that the same data can be presented in a variety of ways. The difference between absorption costing and variable costing is a case in point. The net income of a company can be quite different depending on which method of costing is used. Another example is the means by which a company accounts for inventory. Differences in the Weighted Average method, the First-In, First-Out (FIFO) method, and the Last-In, First-Out (LIFO) method, can dramatically affect a company's bottom line. Finally, the differences in accounting for depreciation can alter the representation of a company's profit because the straight-line method, the double-declining-balance method, the sum-of-the-year's-digits method, and the accelerated cost recovery system each contributes a different amount to total expenses.

I had always believed accounting to be an exact science, and it had not occurred to me that different accounting principles can be applied to the same business to produce different profit reports. As a result of my classes here, I feel more knowledgeable when I examine a company's annual report. I now know to ask questions and to take answers for what they are: one representation of the facts.

At first this inexactness troubled me. However, when I consider the vast variety of businesses in the world and the many different accounting practices that could have evolved, it astonishes me that a great deal of uniformity has arisen.

Finally, regarding Cost Accounting in particular, I have found the idea of variances to be quite interesting. Some accounting procedures seem arcane, and the information presented seems designed primarily for the consumption of other accountants. However, variances seem quite important, and I certainly see the utility of determining where and why a certain production system has failed to yield an expected profit. Though I don't anticipate a career in accounting, I am glad I have been exposed to the idea of variances and think this concept will stand me in good stead in my business career.

—*Gordon Wade Warren*

## *Recipe for a Rice and Shrimp Meal*

The following is an attempt to use an accounting tool for analyzing a non-traditional mode of production: namely, cooking.

A recipe is presented and a breakdown for the costs and benefits has been given. Many assumptions were made about the nature of each ingredient with regard to its nutritional value and consumption during a meal. A calorie/dollar ratio was given. Also, the consumption of calories was provided for each physical activity or chore involved in cooking this meal.

Although the model as presented cannot be used as is to analyze the contribution of each ingredient to the meal, if one could accurately assess the value of each calorie to human life, for example as a percentage of the total daily calorie requirements (perhaps with a sub-group for each food group), this would be a viable model. However, as it stands, the figures are not representative but the concepts are.

*Information and Assumptions*

1. One calorie has a dollar value of $1.
2. Protein has five times the nutrition of carbohydrates.

| | Calories | $ Value | Cost |
|---|---|---|---|
| **Direct Materials** | | | |
| 2 Cups Rice | 400.00 | $400 | $ 2.0 |
| 10 Large Shrimp | 140.00 | $140 | $14.0 |
| | | | |
| **Indirect Materials** | | | |
| Water | 0.00 | $0.00 | $ 0.0 |
| Salt | 0.00 | $0.00 | $ 0.5 |
| | | | |
| **Direct Labor** | | | |
| 6 Minutes Cooking Shrimp | 50.00 | $50 | |
| 10 Minutes Cooking Rice | 30.00 | $30 | |
| 10 Minutes Cleaning Shrimp | 50.00 | $50 | |
| | | | |
| **Indirect Labor** | | | |
| Driving to Store | 30.00 | $30 | |
| Shopping | 50.00 | $50 | |
| | | | |
| **Variable Chores** | | | |
| Serving Each Dish | 50.00 | $50 | |
| Setting the Table | 25.00 | $25 | |
| Doing Dishes | 50.00 | $50 | |
| | | | |
| **Overhead** | | | |
| 20 Min. Electricity For Stove | | | $2.0 |
| 6 Min. Electricity For Stove | | | $0.6 |
| Pot For Cooking Rice | | | $5.0 |
| Pot For Cooking Shrimp | | | $5.0 |
| Shrimp Bamboo Steamer | | | $2.0 |
| | | | |
| **Allocated Consumption** | | | |
| 300 Calories Per | | | |
| Person x 2 | 600.00 | $600 | |

*Traditional Recipe Output*

| | Rice & Shrimp | |
|---|---|---|
| Value | | |
| (Calorie x Nutrition x $) | | 1100.00 |
| Less: Cost of Cooking | | |
| Direct Material | 16.00 | |
| Direct Labor | 130.00 | |
| Overhead | | |
| Indirect Material | 0.50 | |
| Indirect Labor | 80.00 | |
| Electricity | 2.60 | |
| Equipment | 12.00 | 241.10 |
| Gross Value | | 858.90 |
| Less: Chores | 125.00 | |
| Consumption | 600.00 | 725.00 |
| Leftovers | | $133.90 |

*Contribution/Segment Recipe Output*

| | Rice | | Shrimp | | Total |
|---|---|---|---|---|---|
| Value | | | | | |
| (Calorie x Nutrition x $) | 400.00 | | 700.00 | | 1100.00 |
| Less: Variable Cost of Cooking | | | | | |
| Direct Material | 2.00 | | 14.00 | | |
| Direct Labor | 30.00 | | 100.00 | | |
| Variable Overhead | 2.50 | 34.50 | 0.60 | 114.60 | 149.10 |
| Cooking Contribution Margin | | 365.50 | | 585.40 | 950.90 |
| Less: Serving Expenses | | 25.00 | | 25.00 | 50.00 |
| Ingredient Contribution Margin | | $340.50 | | $560.40 | 900.90 |
| Less: Equipment | | | | | 12.00 |
| Common Chores | | | | | 155.00 |
| Allocated Consumption | | | | | 600.00 |
| Leftovers | | | | | $133.90 |

—Dorreya Zaki

## *The Accountant; The Poet*

"How can an accountant be a poet?" you asked;
"How can an accountant not be a poet?" I responded.

The accountant lives in the world of numbers;
Mr. X made two hundred million dollars last year;
Then, he died;
He terminated one thousand employees to increase profits;
Mr. Smith's monthly retirement pay is 100,000 dollars;
The Company lost five billion dollars last year;
The Company terminated fifty thousand employees last year.

Executives are in one corner; workers are in the other corner;
Managers are on one side; unions are on the other side;
The Company is losing billions; unions want more
The Company is losing billions; workers want more;
The Company is in deep trouble; managers want more;
We are in deep trouble.
Managers versus workers; salary versus wage;
Competition; division;
Us versus them;
My team versus their team;
I will win; you will lose;
My parking versus your parking;
My cafeteria versus your cafeteria;
My advantage and your disadvantage;
Is this a business or is this a wrestling match?

The top man earns ten million in this pharmaceutical firm;
His assistant's pay is two million a year;
The assistant to the assistant's pay is a million;
The manager draws a hundred thousand dollars;
The workers survive on ten thousand dollars a year;
Ten thousand were laid off because profits were low;
Because work was scarce;
Because restructuring had helped.

Our cars are gas guzzlers;
Our fireplaces suck the air out of our houses;
We use more energy than any nation on earth;
We spend more money on packaging than anywhere else;
We fill the oceans and the lands with our excessive waste;
We cut trees by thousands;
To build more houses and shopping centers;
More luxury houses for those who have few in the South and North;
More shopping centers than the next generation can fill;
We are leaving the earth in shambles;
We are in deep voodoo!

We send a man to the moon;
We finance a war that costs a billion dollars a day;
Our cities are in shambles;
Inner cities are deteriorating;
Our youth are restless;
AIDS and disease are overwhelming;
And we are in deep voodoo!

We have the old tax law; the new tax law;
The federal tax, the state tax, the city tax, the county tax;
We have vehicle tax, property tax, vehicle tag;
We have the sales tax; the unemployment tax;
Social security tax, medicaid tax; federal income tax;
state income tax; local tax; corporate tax;
And more tax to contend with;
If we learn the loopholes, we can avoid taxes;
If we don't learn the loopholes, we would have evaded the taxes;
If we do it the first way; they will pay us;
If we do it the second way; they would jail us;
And we are in deep voodoo!

There are hundreds of forms to fill out;
SEC forms; IRS forms; DOL forms;
Forms of all sizes;
Forms of all kinds;
More forms than our fathers could even imagine in their dreams;
We spend millions in printing the forms;
We spend billions in filling out the forms;
We are truly in deep voodoo!

We have hundreds of ARB's, APB's, FASB's, and SAS's to deal with;
APB's have superseded ARB's but some are still in force;
FASB's have superseded APB's but some are still in force;
AICPA rulings are obviously in force;
More rules are added every day;
We have thousands of pages of rules;
And you must see to believe the real voodoo!

We don't agree on what we own;
Because our computation depends on the method we use;
Did we use historical costs, replacement costs, cash value?
Did we use market value, residual value, or any other value?
Did we use FIFO, LIFO, WAP, or other methods?
Did we use straight line or some other kind of line?
What kind of allowances do we have?
Where do we show these allowances?
You must be here to see the voodoo!

And you had asked:
"How can an accountant be a poet?"
Tell me:
How can an accountant not be a poet?
Please tell me!

The problems are too complex to solve;
There is so much each person can do;
We must relax and do the best we can;
We must have a sense of humor;
And deal the best with all the voodoo!

How can an accountant be a poet?
How can an accountant not be a poet if he can count?
  —*Roger K. Doost*

## A Business Card

I was a young man, and I thought my job was important;
I had my first business card printed;
It read:
"Chief Plant Accountant & Office Manager, B. F. Goodrich Company."

I left the job to further my education and became more marketable;
I got several degrees after a decade of additional education;
I became a professor.
I hung all my five degrees and five certificates on the wall;
I neatly put all the books on the bookshelves;
The books that I had read and the ones I hadn't read;
And I had another business card printed:
It read:
"DPA meaning doctorate in public administration;
MBA which means masters in business administration;
MACC meaning masters in accountancy;
CPA which means certified public accountant;
CMA meaning certified management accountant;
Associate Professor,
Clemson University."

A decade passed;
I learned I do not know what I thought I knew;
I thought there are many more things that I don't know;
I learned that I should announce what I don't know;
I should not dwell on the little I once knew.

My new business card reads:
"Roger K. Doost,
A world citizen,
And a student."

Now that the ego has stepped aside;
I think I can understand myself;
I think I can understand others;
I think I will be a better person;
I think I will be a better servant of the human race;
I think the world will be a better place.
        —Roger K. Doost

## *The Uninvited Plants*

In the early morning
of a pleasantly crisp
and cool day of spring
I stand in my garden
enjoying my handiwork
of trees, lawns, vegetables, and flowers
neatly arranged,
in orderly, equal distances,
just like I had planned.

Admiring the rows of tulips
I see an uninvited petunia in their midst,
and, tending the cucumbers
I notice an unexpected pansy looking at me
with apologetic eyes.

I go to the patio
to get the weed puller
to pull out the uninvited,
thinking:
I must safeguard and protect
the order and arrangement of my landscape.

Returning to the garden I notice
even another uninvited guest:
a plant whose name
I don't even know,
staring at me
from under the stairs.

I am suddenly reminded
of the garden of life:
no matter how well we plan it,
there are always uninvited, and
unexpected events and accidents.

We can't avoid them.
We let them live on their term.
We accept them,
sometimes even with gratitude,
letting them teach us
new lessons on life.

I put the tools back in the patio,
letting my uninvited plants to live their term,
in appreciation of the wonderful lesson
they have just taught me.
                —*Tahirih Foroughi*

## The Tea Party

*To my mother*

I am sitting in my living room
sipping tea.

a most delicious tea
a most pleasing tea
a most refreshing tea

a tea with the sweet scent of roses
a tea with the romantic aroma of honeysuckles
a tea with the refreshing smell of orange
a tea with the wonderful fragrance of jasmines

I am drinking tea

a tea touched by the gentle presence of cardamom
a tea fostered with the excitement of cinnamon
a tea educated with the excellence of saffron
a tea remarked with a tender touch of mint

I am having tea, sip-by-sip

a tea sweetened with the sugar of love
a tea seasoned with the spice of kindness
a tea strengthened with the honey of affinity

a tea rainbowed with the saffron of friendship
a tea nurtured with the advice of afffection
a tea disciplined with
        just an air of the bitterness of concern

I am enjoying my tea.

a tea blended in the blender of unity
a tea matured in the container of modesty
a tea packed with the hands of motherhood
a tea submitted through the mail of submission
a tea brewed in the teapot of tranquility
        on the gentle fire of harmony
a tea poured into the cup of memories
the WONDERFUL SWEET memories of my BELOVED MOTHER.

She sent me this tea from Persia.
in a small container
fifteen years ago.

Alas. Alas. she passed away five years later

This tea is an example of my mother.
Every time I drink this tea.
I learn a new lesson of life.

Just like my beloved mother.
It teaches me a new lesson. each time.

Every single time I was with her
she taught me a lesson of life
by her example. not by words.

I have made many cups of this tea
but, just like my mother
and her unforgettable example of excellence
        in deeds and words.

and, just like her unforgettable kindness and gentleness.
her tea has continued to exist and to be with me.

I have had numerous Tea Parties with her tea.
both alone or with family and friends.

In these tea parties I have felt my mother
and she has touched me.

I have extended my mother's tea
by adding new tea to the jar
and, by blending and mixing the new tea
very well
with the original tea.

and I intend to continue this process
forever.
as long as I live.

Thus, she will be with me
any time I give a TEA PARTY.

You are certainly welcome to join me.
　　　—*Tahirih Foroughi*

## *Account of Life*

To: My *father*

It is a hot summer afternoon
in Glendale, Arizona

they are sitting row after row
like soldiers in the field

they are all students
taking a cost accounting exam.

I can see the worry
the tiredness
the anxiousness
the fear of the unknown results
mixed feelings about the subject matter
hesitation about the correct answers
and many other questions
on their faces

they are so quiet
as though
they are in a temple
meditating

they have to work on every single item
hoping
that their balance sheet
will balance

they have to measure
the actual results
vs. the standard expectations
and
the expenses
vs. the income
so that their income statement
        shows the true results

to pass this course
they need
perseverance and hard work
Life is no different from accounting

to succeed in life
you have to work hard
you have to be honest and truthful
you have to be up-to-date
you have to work through weaknesses to become strong
you have to persevere
you have to accept
        and be ready for
        ups and downs of life

to have a balanced balance sheet in life
you need to make sure that:
        you are a well-rounded and balanced person
        you are well-informed
        you start the year with a balanced situation
        you establish standards for yourself
        and you follow those standards
        you are friendly and wise, at the same time
        and you keep track
        not only of your assets
        but also of your liabilities

and to have a good income statement of life
you need to:
      be truthful
      be hard-working
      know your environmental conditions
      stay away from desire
      don't buy more than you can sell or use
      let your conscience be your reward
      keep your life's account simple and straightforward
      and don't be afraid of questions and tests
      and keep track of your revenues and expenses

This is a lesson for life
LEARN IT
      —*Tahirih Foroughi*

## *The Same Essence*

*Dedicated to Thunderbird*

We are all human
and
we come from the same essence.

We belong to the same globe,
the small globe called Earth.
Why do we act like enemies?

No animal kills its own kind.
Why do we massacre
our own: the humankind?

We are the fruits
of the same tree,
the flowers
of the same garden,
and
the citizens
of the same country:
the Earth.

No matter
what ethnic, religious, geographic,
racial or national background
we come from,
we are the inhabitants
of the same land:
the Earth.

If we are:
black,
red,
white,
or yellow,
we are the four qualities
of the same Essence.

Let us wash away
our differences
and cooperate,
since:
we are members of
the same family:
the family of Humankind,
and
we are campers
in the same desert:
the Earth.

So,
let us work for peace,
let us work for cooperation,
let us work for harmony,
let us work for unity,
let us work for friendship.
—*Tahirih Foroughi,*
  *translated from and inpired by a poem written by*
  *the early twentieth-century Persian poet, Naeem.*

## *January Became February*

January became February and my respite became 15 hours,
after a 5 hour flight the bare eastern trees became new cactus flowers

My first day in Cost Accounting will not be forgotten,
as I realized my 1982 Principles had been forgotten!

I worked hard out of fear,
only to awaken near the rear

I knew that this first test was not the very end,
but also knew that my skills would need a mend

I also came to believe in the value of this class they called Cost,
that if I could only work smarter, all would not be lost

My pencils grew duller, my calculator came to smoke,
the tunnel light I could see as I continued to poke

My dreams were of job order and process, standard and actual,
the variances I thought of, even in classes not so factual

The exams they improved, gradually but sure,
the kind teacher showed pity, realizing there must be a cure

And although the grades are not in, I have come to the conclusion,
the understanding of Cost is a valuable qualification.
    *—Daniel K. Usher*

## *A Higher Realm*

I am sitting in the airport
watching the crowd
and
waiting for my flight.

We are called to board
the airliner

I approach the gate.

I should be happy
but
I feel sad.

Sitting in my seat
I look through the window,
but I can't see anything.

The airliner is immersed
in heavy fog
and clouds.

After some waiting
we take off.

We are now
high in the sky
but,
there are clouds everywhere
and, it is dark
inside and out…

I feel like an earthly being
who cannot see
or even visualize
the next world
the higher realm.

I feel cheated and ignorant
about inside and outside
the clouds.

I feel cheated and ignorant
about this realm of dust
and
the Higher Realm.

Suddenly
the airliner
breaks out of the heavy clouds.

Now, there is sunshine everywhere
I feel happy, warm and delighted.

Suddenly
I hear a voice
My inner voice
saying:

Now, clouds of ignorance
are lifted
and,
rays of the sun of
joy and balance
will make you warm.

I feel happy and content
and come to the
realization
that:
 The Higher Realm is within me
 It is my inner voice
 Only if I
 carefully
 listen to it.
 —*Tahirih Foroughi*

## Cost Accounting Is a Pleasure

*This book is dedicated to the memory of Charles Olin Norton.*

Cost accounting is a pleasure
For which there is no measure,
It's such an efficient way
To keep one's costs at bay.

There is, however, one aspect
upon which when I reflect
I'd love to be able to change
To give it a relevant range.

Sometimes it is so confusing
So as to be amusing,
'Cause there are so many different Joes
Among the problem solving pros.

I would really love to find
A way to avoid the grind,
Words like contribution margin
And all the accounting jargon,
Confuse me in such a way
That I don't know what to say.

When it comes to ratios
And how the business goes,
I can understand
The entire business plan.

But when it comes to variance
and the efficiency of firms,
I can only think of deviance
And my wish to avoid the term.

Yet after every class
my confusion seems to pass,
And I can say with zest
Dr. Foroughi is the best.
            —*Charles Norton*

# CONCLUSION: *Like a Complete Work of Art*

As mentioned in the Introduction to this book, Charles Olin Norton, to whose memory this book is dedicated, was our son. Charles' death occurred as the result of a bicycle accident. He had been an amateur bicycle racer during his school and college years and had continued to ride for exercise and pleasure while at Thunderbird. On one of his frequent excursions he was hit by a motor home and killed.

## *The How-Question:*

The two questions raised by such an untimely death are: how and why did it happen? The how-question asks that death be explained and, thereby, made understandable, and is answered by a factually descriptive explanation. This is indicated by our use of the phrase, "the reason *for* his death," when asking for the cause of a person's death. Such a question is in principle conclusive and in the great majority of cases can be satisfied. Furthermore, we do not speak of "the reason *of* his death" in asking and answering the how-question, because "explanation" is not of the essence and nature of death. To treat death in this way would be to reduce it to an explanation, extraneous to its nature, essence, and significance. Rather, it is applied to the event of death, understood as the effect of a cause. A rational explanation is not *of* death—does not belong to the nature of death—but is *for* death—is applied to the event of death: an explanation would explain away death's *essential* significance by replacing it with an abstraction.

On the other hand, the why-question addresses the question of the meaning, or rather the *significance*, of life and death, and, therefore, it cannot be answered in the same way as the how-question. This is because meaning, understood as significance, is not an empirical reality and, therefore, is neither factually descriptive, as the meaning of a true or false descriptive sentence, nor the conclusion of a rational explanation. Consequently, the why-question is different in kind from the how-question, thus requiring a different kind of answer from a simple explanation.

The significance of Life is generally understood in terms of "purpose" and of death in terms of "completion"—the completion of one's life. Furthermore, "purpose" is understood in two different ways: as a single, specific purpose for a particular person's life or as an unspecified general concept of purpose, which is true of life in general—of the life of any and every person. This distinction is reflected in the expression, "the purpose *for* his life," regarding the former, and by the phrase, "the purpose *of* his life," regarding the latter. To speak of "the purpose *of* life" is to understand this unspecified and general purpose to be of the essence and significance of human Life in general. In addition, to speak of "the completion of life," as "fulfilled purpose," is to understand "completion" to be of the essence and significance of human Death in general. We cannot identify a person's entire lifetime with any single particular purpose, and, therefore, we cannot identify his death with a single particular fulfilled purpose. Thus, it follows that we cannot answer the why-question—why did he die?—by an explanation, because the reason, required by the explanation, would have to be formulated in terms of a single specific fulfilled purpose, which is not available.

This kind of answer becomes many answers and is in principle not conclusive because we cannot determine any one specific purpose—or whether it has been fulfilled—in any particular person's life, as signaled by his death. People voice many different purposes throughout the duration of their lives. The fulfillment of them, and, therefore, of their lives, is offered as the reason for their deaths and, thereby, gives their lives and deaths a variety of explanations and significances.

Furthermore, people die before any conceivable purpose could have been fulfilled, and, so, there can be no possible significance of, or explanation for, their lives or deaths. Also, there are people who continue to live long after any conceivable purpose has been fulfilled, so, again, there is no possible reason, no possible significance of, or explanation for, their lives and deaths. Therefore, we must conclude that a rational explanation, giving a descriptive answer to the why-question, is impossible, thus ruling out the use of the phrase "the purpose *for* his life or death" as appropriate to the why-question.

Finally, we may only speak of "the purpose *of* his life or death" in reference to asking and answering the why-question, because here "purpose" is used as an unspecified general concept and refers to the essence and significance of Life, as well as of an individual's life, and similarly "fulfilled purpose" refers to the essence and significance of Death, as well as of an individual's death. In contrast, the reason given, as an explanation and answer to the how-question, functions as either the cause or the effect of a causal relation between the events of one's life and death, as is indicated by the phrase "the reason *for* his life or death."

A person's lifetime, existence has a beginning, a middle, and an end, which are his birth, his lifetime, and his death; there is no individual life without birth and death, and there is neither birth nor death without life. The three form a whole and must be understood as a whole, not separately or individually: each must be seen as necessarily involving the other two. To do so is to understand the *significance* of both birth and death in terms of the particular relation that each has to life. Since, on the level of the why-question, life is understood as *purpose, their significance is their relation to that purpose:* birth is (life of) potential purpose and death is (of life of) fulfilled purpose. Therefore, the two opposites of birth and death are held together and receive their significance by their dialectical relationship, understood in terms of a shared purpose, that is, a shared life, acting as their common ground.

On the other hand, on the level of the how-question, the explanation for the *events* of birth and death is the nature of the relation that each has to a person's physical existence. Since his physical life is one of coming into existence and going out of existence—of waxing and waning, generation and degeneration—*the explanation for birth and death is the relationship that each has to the growth and decay of the physical body:* birth/conception is the cause of physical existence, which is understood as its effect, and death is the effect of a decaying material body, which is understood as its cause. Therefore, on the level of cause and effect of rational explanation, birth is initial and death is terminal; there can be no end without a beginning and no beginning without an end, which is to say that there can be no effect without a cause and no cause without an effect. Thus, the two opposites are held together and explained by a causal relationship, as their common link, in which a shared physical life and existence is both effect and cause.

The difference between the how- and why-questions is qualitative: the former is a human question, having its source in the understanding, and is answered by human reason, whereas the latter is a divine question, which is spoken and answered in the heart. It is also addressed and answered by one or the other or both of two options: either by the claims or promises of a religious tradition or by an analogy to Art. For both options the explanation required and offered by human reason is not forthcoming. In place of "understanding," understood as the knowledge of explanation, there is a knowledge, for which no explanation or definition is possible. For both Religion and Art, this latter kin of knowledge is understood to be insight or discernment, called Wisdom, the substance of which is Truth. In religion Truth takes the form of the moral Good—faith in the ultimate goodness of the divine will. In art Truth takes the form of aesthetic Beauty—belief in the transforming power of great works of Art. For both of these options knowledge flows from faith or belief, and informs the heart, not the understanding. Such knowledge has its source in that Truth, *by which we know* and which is a mystery, being self-authenticating and transforming power. The Truth of Wisdom makes sense of that which cannot be understood—for which there is no explanation. To know in this way is *not* to know any*thing*, neither physical or mental objects nor physical or mental events, but to know *knowing*: to be grasped by an Intelligence—Intelligibility Itself—which gives significance to and makes sense of the intellectually and rationally meaningless, insignificant, and senseless.

Finally, a person lives on two levels: the level of the Spirit—a life of significance and purpose—which is the ontological level of Being; and the level of the physical—an existence of cause and effect and rational reflection—which is the existential level of explanation. Thus, one lives simultaneously in Heaven and on Earth. The answer to the question "How did Charles die?" is that, due to the injuries he sustained from his accident, his body could no longer adequately function and, therefore, could no longer be host to the Spirit of Life. On the other hand, the answer to the question "Why did Charles die?" is that he was born and that his life, physical existence, necessarily involved birth as well as death and death as well as birth; the reality and significance of his death depends upon the reality and significance of his birth, as its opposite. The reality and significance of each is mutually dependent upon the other; without death birth is meaningless, of no significance, and without birth death is meaningless, of no significance. And the answer to the question "Why did he die so young?" is that his life was complete, its purpose was fulfilled. Therefore, his birth and death were also satisfied, because when seen as a whole, birth and death are essentially one and the same—two aspects of the same reality: their reality and significance are the reality and significance of the common life which they share, as its two aspects. One's life points simultaneously in two opposite directions: to birth and death, thus holding them in a balance of wholeness. By embracing both birth and death, Life transcends the opposition between them and, thus, by resolving and overcoming their opposition, Life absorbs birth and death into Itself, thus transforming them into new Life.

We would like to conclude this section with a crude, yet simple, analogy. The relationship between a person's physical existence, in the form of a material body, and his ontological reality, in the form of a spiritual life, is analogous to the relationship between an electric motor, with all its material components, and the electric current, by which it runs and becomes "alive."

The motor and current exist independently; the current is available both before and after the existence of the motor. Furthermore, the motor can only run when it is in good physical order and when it is supplied with the current; remove the current and the motor stops running—is "dead"—or damage one or more of the components of the motor and it "dies." Relative to the existence, or "lifetime," of the motor, the current is eternal. Although it may appear to, the current does not come into and go out of existence as the motor does; that is, the current does not disappear, or lose its reality, and in this analogy represents the ontological order of being, Spirit/Life, rather than the existential order of existence, matter.

And so it is with a person: relative to the existence, or lifetime, of his body, Spirit/Life is eternal. Although it may appear so, Spirit/Life does not come into and go out of existence as his body does, as determined by his birth and death. Spirit/Life does not gain or lose its reality; rather, the body does. The reality of a person's Spirit/Life is of the order of being, not that of existence. Just as the electric current is transformed into an electromagnetic field of force, by which the motor runs, so a person's Spirit/Life is transformed into human consciousness, by which his body is made alive and lives.

## The Why-Question and Its Two Options

In order to avoid the inconclusive nature of the why-question and to give it in principle a conclusive answer, we trust the significance of Charles' life and death to be an expression of the divine will. In addition, we believe the significance of his life and death to be analogous to that of a work of art. Thereby we discern the answer to the question of their significance, as it is given in both of the above two options. However, for the purposes of this Introduction, we shall speak of Charles' life and death metaphorically, as a work of art. Such a metaphor avoids the need to posit a reason in the form of either a specific cause or a specific purpose, either of which would be extraneous to the significance of his life and death, as well as to that of a work of art.

A work of art is a unity of a beginning, a middle, and an end and has an integrity of balance, as realized by wholeness and completeness. The artist discerns when the work of art is complete and finished, not rationally or descriptively, not in any quantitative or measurable sense, but intuitively, as the response of his whole being to the work and as expressed by "Ah, good: that's it—finished!" with no explanation offered. For no such explanation is called for or necessary, even if one *were* possible. To add more strokes to the canvas, notes to the score, words to the manuscript, or carvings to the stone would only compromise the unity of the work and, thus, violate its integrity. The former work would no longer be and its own unique significance would be lost; it would either be a different work or no work at all.

The significance of a work of art is the work of art; it has no other significance. It is not necessary to discern or understand its significance in terms of purposes or anything else, such as the materials used, the period in which it was created, or the name, nationality, or age of the artist, because each such item is an addition and is extraneous to the painting, concerto, poem, or sculpture. It was due to the violation of this principle, during the periods of the Nazi and Communist regimes, that Art suffered a decline in Germany and the Soviet Union; it became a means to an extraneous end, rather than an end in itself. It is by this principle that a frame for a painting, silence for a concerto or poem, and space for a sculpture or a work of architecture have their significance, namely, to set aside the work of art from all that is extraneous to it. For it is a new creation, unique and sufficient unto itself: a universe of its own being in Truth and significance. Furthermore, the significance of a work of art is not the conclusion of a rational process; rather, it is a gift, given gratuitously: a treasure, found or discovered, and to be received, contemplated, embraced, and entered into.

And so it is with Life. The person also has his "frame," "silence," or "space," which, as his quiet inner center of stillness and silence, is the true center of his being. It is *this* center, which separates him from the fragmented and chaotic outer world, which is a reflection of the false centers of the self-centered egos of people in conflict: dreaming and trying to be what they are not and cannot be, thus causing frustration, confusion, anger, hatred, and violence. For it is the world within, which is the locus of a person's being and the source of his significance, the significance which announces who he is and which is the only significance he has. His life is his significance and his significance is his life: they are of the very essence and nature of his being, not of his existence. A person's being determines his existential life of attitudes and actions, which are the outer speech of his inner life, just as the paint on the canvas, the notes in the score, the words in the manuscript, and the cuttings in the stone are metaphorically an "outer speech," expressing the significance of the work of art. The earthly life of a person's physical existence is a window or icon through which one has a momentary glimpse into his significance and inner being.

The degree of balance realized in a life and a work of art is the measure of their wholeness and is, also, the measure of the degree to which their essential unity is realized. The oneness of the inner being of the individual life and of the particular work of art is the source of their essential unity, integrity, and significance, as expressed by their wholeness and completeness. Their integrity is the integration of their essential oneness and their existential wholeness, which is achieved by the resolution of the tension of the pairs of opposites: the unity of the ontological and the existential, of Being and doing, as well as of birth and death, freedom and bondage, joy and pain, peace and anxiety, the lost and the redeemed, the individual and the community. The essential, pre-existent oneness at the center of Life and Art is, thus, uncovered and expressed, as their significance.

To ask why a young person should prematurely die is to ask either for the reason *for* his death or for the significance *of* his death. The former form of the why-question has no single conclusive answer. Therefore, we do not ask why Charles died at twenty-seven years of age, because to do so is to open Pandora's box, as well as to look for the answer to the latter form of the question—the question of the significance of his life and death—in a place other than the essential nature of his life and death, themselves. Rather, their significance is of the essential nature of all Life and all Death.

To ask the latter form is to see the significance of Charles' life in terms of its quality, not its quantity—not its brevity—and is to speak of it in terms analogous to those applied to a work of art. The significance of a work of art is the work itself, independent of the circumstances of its creation, such as the name of the artist, the date and time of year created, or the materials used. A work of art is a work of art, whether its creation took a few weeks, as did Handel's *Messiah*, or a few years, as did Brahms' *First Symphony*. We know and discern its significance by either engaging or entering into it, by either the performance or contemplation of it: we know the significance by knowing the work, and we know the work by knowing the significance. They are one and the same.

To speak of people's lives as works of art is to imagine the world in which they live to be a vast school of art, the classrooms of which are studios, each for a particular art work: music, painting, sculpture, literature, theater. The people of the world are the students, and the principal of the school is the Master Artist, who oversees their work. Having encouraged and instructed them, the Master creates artists, who become works of art in themselves. The piece of art that a student works with, of whatever material, is a symbol of his own life, as a work of art. Upon completing the piece, the student graduates from the school, regardless of his age.

The classrooms of the school become filled with a variety of kinds of art at various stages of completion and of various degrees of excellence. As is the case with a work of art, a person's life has balance, harmony, and proportion, different degrees of which result in different degrees of wholeness, completion, and perfection. The students are of a variety of ages, at various stages of training, and have different kinds and degrees of talent. Each work represents the stage of completion and degree of excellence of the life of a student. It is our own lives, with the assistance of the Master, that we are fashioning into proportionate and balanced wholes, the completeness of which is the signature of their unity and integrity. Some excellent works are completed in a short time, and their creators, who have discerned their gifts and have followed the guidance of the Master, have graduated and left the school with his blessing.

To speak of a person's life as a work of art is to understand it in terms of the aesthetic category of Beauty, which involves proportion and harmony, balance and wholeness, thus pointing to the inner unity and outer integrity of the person. And to do so is to see the person's life in moral, as well as aesthetic, terms: for both the moral Good and the aesthetic Beauty, aspects of that Truth which is one, reflect the ontological oneness at the center of Life and Art, as manifested in both their individual and mutual unity and integrity. The outer relationships of proportion and harmony, balance and wholeness *among* people signify the inner unity and outer integrity of individuals in community and of community of individuals: such individuals are just and righteous, and such a community is one of order and harmony as well as justice and righteousness. Moreover, a person's behavior is a reflection of his character, of his inner being: a beautiful life is a good life and a good life is a beautiful life. Beauty and Good are synonymous; one cannot be without the other. They are also synonymous with Truth, in the sense that each is an aspect of that Truth which is One: the Truth that is both Beauty *and* Good. Life's significance and purpose, as the presupposition and substance of the why-question and answer, have their source in that Truth, which is ontological, not factual, is intuitive, not discursive, is self-authenticating, not inferential, and arises in and flows from the heart, not the head.

## Summary and Conclusion

We have seen that the how-question, with its answer, is peripheral to a discussion of Dr. Foroughi's vision of Life. Her vision sees unity and integrity to be at the heart and of the essential nature of all life. This vision of the oneness of Life is expressed by the balance of all pairs of opposites, thus acknowledging all of life and resulting in the wholeness and completeness of all life: the individual and the community, the good and the bad, liberty and law, right and wrong, chaos and order, the beautiful and the ugly. These are the terms in which the significance of one's life and death is made intelligible and, in turn, the why-question as well, thus placing the why-question, with its answer, at the heart of Dr. Foroughi's vision. The presence of this essential oneness, as the source of the unity and integrity of one's life, is at the center of every person's life. Therefore, it is in our hearts that the divine question is spoken, heard, and answered.

We have seen that we cannot answer the why-question in terms of a purpose for life which would be single and specific for any and every particular person; to do so would be to treat the answer to the why-question as an explanation and, thus, to confuse its *significance* with the *meaning* of the how-question. Therefore, we have understood the why-question in terms of the purpose of Life and have understood "purpose," as an unspecified general concept, which is of the essence of all life and, therefore, true of the

78

lives of any and all people. It is in this sense that "purpose" is used in the spiritual option, where a person's life is understood to be complete when its purpose is fulfilled, as signaled by his death. Here "purpose" means to realize a life of wholeness and completeness, unity and integrity, by embracing all aspects of one's life, whether "good" or "bad": birth and death, joy and pain, freedom and bondage, peace and anxiety, order and chaos, liberty and law, the individual and the community, as well as the ontological and the factual aspects of being and existing, respectively. To do otherwise would be to deny half of life as being bad and to accept the remaining half as being good, thus living a partial life of imbalance. All the opposites are aspects of Life, which is informed by and has the power of the Spirit to realize its essential oneness by going beyond the opposites, transforming and absorbing them into "new" Life, for which there is neither "good" nor "bad": neither individual nor society, liberty nor law, right nor wrong, chaos nor order, beauty nor ugliness, birth nor death, joy nor pain, freedom nor bondage, peace nor anxiety, as well as neither the ontological nor the existential, Being nor existence—neither Heaven nor Earth. For we are called "to be": to receive, embrace, enter into, offer up all of our lives, as sacred, and, thereby, we are to be transformed—made whole, one, and new.

On the other hand, for the purposes of this article, it is in neither of the above two senses of "purpose" that the art option is available and relevant to the why-question. This is because we have chosen not to understand the significance of Art in terms of purpose or fulfilled purpose: neither in the sense of the purpose *for* art nor in the sense of the purpose *of* art. For the art option, a work of art is understood to be complete when all its opposites are embraced and in balance, thus resulting in harmony, proportion, and wholeness and expressing the essential unity, integrity, and oneness of its being and, similarly, of the being of an individual's life. As is the case with a person's life, the significance of a work of art is intuited, discerned, "known," as a quality of one's experience of it: of one's performing, reciting, or contemplating it. The conflicts, issues, contradictions, disorder, confusion, chaos, and brokenness of man's existence, both individually and socially, are overcome and resolved in Art; in all great works of art, the tension of the opposites, embraced and held in balance, is overcome and resolved, mysteriously transformed into a new creation. Therefore, the essential Nature and Power of Art to resolve and replace disorder by order, conflict by harmony, imbalance by balance, brokenness by wholeness, is what makes it an image of the essential Nature and Spirit of Life. It is a divine moment of Transformation, Creation, and Mystery: an Icon of a New Heaven and a New Earth.

So we dare not ask the why-question, unless we are prepared to go beyond human reason and explanation, and to look for its significance and answer in another world. For it is a divine question in the sense that it has a divine answer, both of which are addressed and satisfied by Religion and Art, as expressions of a single Truth. To ask the question from within a human frame of reference is to insist that the question of the significance of Life and Death, an ontological question of Truth, be answered as if it were of the same logical status as the existential how-question of cause and effect. But the why-question, being of the heart and not of the head, has its own "reasons," which are also of the heart and not of the head.

So, where do we go for the divine answer? We go to one or the other—or both—of the religion and art options. According to the analogy for an individual life provided by the art option, we go to the life of the one who has left us. It is there that we find the answer, as the significance of his life. The life of the person whose death has posed the why-question is both question and answer, in the sense that a person's life is its own significance: if a life is its own significance, then one life is only a single significance. Furthermore, if a person's life is a single significance, which is both question and answer, then there is no point in asking the question and insisting on an answer, because there is no distinction between them: they are identical, and therefore meaningless, *as question and answer.*

We do not ask the question "Why is the Mona Lisa finished or complete?", for to do so would be to ask "Why is there the Mona Lisa?", because for it to be finished is for it to be: it cannot be finished without being, and it cannot be without being finished. Therefore, there is no why-question to ask, because the question itself presupposes its very own answer: namely, that there is a Mona Lisa. Further, the why-question cannot even be thought, unless the Mona Lisa be: to be finished is to be complete, and to be complete is to be finished. Why is the Mona Lisa finished? It is finished because it is complete, which is to say that it is finished because it is finished: the question is the answer and the answer is the question.

Likewise, the significance of a person's life is the voice of the spirit of his life, which speaks with one voice and is the Spirit that informs all life. The significance of one's life is the message of the Spirit to those who have ears that hear and eyes that see: who hear the voice and see the vision of the heart. The Spirit from within the heart speaks the message, of which the voice and the vision are one and the same. A person's life, *as a work of art,* has already announced that the significance of his death is that of his life and that the significance of his life is that of his death: since the significance is one and is both question and answer, the answer to the question posed by death is the question and the question is the answer. Thus has the spirit informed hearing ears and seeing eyes by its declaration of Truth:

"ALL IS WELL!"

> —*Howard George Norton*
> *Ann Fisher Norton*
> *December 1993*
> *Baltimore*